Tricky GRAMMAR

Grade 5

by Alex Shirran and Jennifer Sun

Carson-Dellosa Publishing LLC
Greensboro, North Carolina

Credits

Content Editor: Ginny Swinson

Copy Editor: Carrie D'Ascoli

Layout and Cover Design: Lori Jackson

Cover Art and Inside Illustrations: Nick Greenwood

This book has been correlated to state, common core state, national, and Canadian provincial standards. Visit *www.carsondellosa.com* to search for and view its correlations to your standards.

Carson-Dellosa Publishing LLC
PO Box 35665
Greensboro, NC 27425 USA
www.carsondellosa.com

Printed in the USA • All rights reserved.
1 2 3 4 5 HPS 15 14 13 12 11

ISBN 978-1-936024-27-8
335101151

Table of Contents

Tricky Grammar **takes a unique approach to grammar instruction**—it makes grammar fun, quirky, and sometimes hilarious! *Tricky Grammar* perfectly balances high-interest, cross-curricular text with a traditional, rules-based approach to grammar.

Students will love being led through activities by a host of grammar gremlins that point out each trick, trap, and technicality of grammar. *Tricky Grammar* piques student interest by incorporating grammar rules with amazing and sometimes shocking trivia, weird science, captivating history tidbits, and silly jokes.

The rules of grammar are clearly stated in simplified language and presented in easy-to-understand units. Each page begins with an over-arching grammar statement followed by one or more practical bulleted rules. At least one example accompanies each rule and models how the rule applies in a sentence. Then, engaging activities and fun factoids motivate students to improve their grammar skills as they strive for academic success.

Tricky Grammar **will enhance students' communication skills through the following:**

- Each activity adapts to large-group, small-group, or individual presentation.

- Grammar rules and definitions are stated at the top of each page for clarity and reference, and these rules are frequently repeated using different sentence patterns to reinforce students' comprehension.

- Each skill is modeled using interesting, authentic text to keep students motivated.

- The activities use engaging and amusing facts to challenge students and improve grammar skills.

With these features, *Tricky Grammar* will become your favorite easy-to-use source for grammar practice:

- More than 100 fact-filled activity pages make *Tricky Grammar* ideal for daily classroom exercises or at-home review.

- Each unit (*Parts of Speech and Word Study*, *Grammar Usage*, *Grammar and Writing*, and *Punctuation*) is designed to be used either sequentially or to target individual skills.

- Activity content correlates to state and national science, social studies, and language arts standards.

- A two-page skills matrix quickly identifies each page's particular focus.

- Grammar gremlins animate each page with conversational tips and quips.

- Factoids and joke breaks illustrate grammar rules in action—and factoids can be used as part of the assignment or read just for fun!

Skills Matrix

Page Number	Grammar		Usage				Composition: Sentence Structure			Composition: Paragraphs		Mechanics and Vocabulary			
	Parts of Speech	Parts or Types of Sentences	Agreement	Pronoun Usage	Verb Usage	Modifiers	Formal & Informal Writing	Complete Sentences	Sentence Revision	Parts of a Paragraph	The Whole Composition	Capitalization	Punctuation	Word Study	Spelling
9	•											•			
10	•														
11	•														
12	•	•		•		•							•		
13	•														•
14	•														•
15	•														•
16	•														•
17	•												•		•
18	•												•		•
19	•				•										
20	•				•										
21	•				•										•
22	•				•										
23	•				•										•
24	•				•										
26	•					•									
27	•					•						•			
28	•					•									
29	•					•									•
30	•					•									•
31	•					•									
32	•					•									
33	•					•									•
35	•			•											
36	•			•											
37	•			•											
38	•			•											
39	•			•											
41	•														
42	•														
43	•	•													
44	•	•													
45	•	•													
46	•	•													
48														•	
49														•	
50		•						•							
51		•											•		
52		•						•							
53		•			•			•							
54		•						•							
55	•	•													
56	•	•													
57		•						•	•				•		
58		•						•	•						
60	•			•									•		•
61	•	•	•												
62	•	•	•												
63	•	•	•												

Skills Matrix

Page Number	Grammar		Usage				Composition: Sentence Structure			Composition: Paragraphs		Mechanics and Vocabulary			
	Parts of Speech	Parts or Types of Sentences	Agreement	Pronoun Usage	Verb Usage	Modifiers	Formal & Informal Writing	Complete Sentences	Sentence Revision	Parts of a Paragraph	The Whole Composition	Capitalization	Punctuation	Word Study	Spelling
64	•	•	•	•											
65	•	•	•	•											
66	•	•	•	•											
68	•					•									
69	•					•									
70									•					•	
71	•				•										
72	•				•										
73	•				•										
74														•	•
75														•	•
76		•													
77						•	•		•						
78							•		•						
79		•					•		•						
80		•					•	•	•				•		
81		•						•	•			•	•		
82		•						•	•				•		
83		•					•	•	•						
85						•			•						
86						•			•						
87	•			•											
88			•		•				•						
89	•		•	•					•						
90									•						
92		•					•						•		
93							•		•						
94							•			•	•				
95							•			•	•				
96		•					•			•	•				
97		•					•			•	•				
98							•								
99							•								
100	•	•										•			
101												•			
102												•	•		
103		•											•		
104		•											•		
105													•		
106													•		
107		•											•		
108		•											•		
110	•												•		•
111													•		
112							•						•		
113		•											•	•	
114	•					•							•	•	•
115	•					•							•	•	
116													•		

Pretest

Circle the letter of each correct answer.

1. Which is a run-on sentence?

   A. Adult kangaroos can jump more than 25 feet (98 m) with each jump.

   B. The temperature of outer space is -54°F (-270°C), and outer space is a vacuum.

   C. Some hummingbirds are so small that one of their enemies is an insect.

   D. People have a tailbone at the end of their spine, it is called a coccyx.

2. What type of sentence is this?
Did you know that special neurons in your skin send messages to your brain at more than 150 miles (241 km) per hour?

   A. declarative

   B. exclamatory

   C. interrogative

   D. imperative

3. Which sentence is in the present tense?

   A. In 1770, Lieutenant James Cook ran his ship on top of the Great Barrier Reef, but he managed to free the vessel.

   B. To use her long canine teeth, a saber-toothed cat will open her mouth up to 120 degrees wide.

   C. Lava was spewing from the fissure in the ground.

   D. Most dreams occur during the rapid eye movement (REM) stage of sleep.

4. Which is the simple subject of the sentence?
Found in Russia, the deepest lake in the world is 5,715 feet (1,742 m) deep.

   A. Found in Russia

   B. lake

   C. the deepest lake

   D. in the world

5. Which is the complete predicate?
Most major league baseball bats are manufactured from ash wood.

   A. Most major league baseball bats

   B. are manufactured

   C. ash wood

   D. are manufactured from ash wood

6. Which is the indirect object?
France gave the United States the Statue of Liberty in 1884.

   A. France

   B. gave

   C. the United States

   D. the Statue of Liberty

Pretest

Circle the letter of each correct answer.

7. Which is the direct object?
Half of the world's population has never made or received a phone call.

- A. population
- B. never
- C. phone
- D. call

8. What is the mistake in the sentence?
The U.S. Department of Defense are the largest employer in the country.

- A. misplaced modifier
- B. subject-verb agreement
- C. dangling modifier
- D. sentence fragment

9. Which words are adjectives?
Coral reefs require clear, unpolluted water at temperatures of 64.4°F (18°C) or above.

- A. coral and reefs
- B. clear and unpolluted
- C. reefs, water, and temperatures
- D. coral, clear, and unpolluted

10. Which word is an adverb?
Many people do not realize that unpasteurized milk can cause very serious health risks.

- A. realize
- B. very
- C. serious
- D. risks

11. Which is the dependent clause?
When a person is choking on a piece of food, one first aid strategy is to perform the Heimlich maneuver.

- A. When a person is choking on a piece of food
- B. one first aid strategy
- C. one first aid strategy is to perform the Heimlich maneuver
- D. a piece of food

12. What is the mistake in the sentence?
A person is born with two kidneys, but you can live with just one.

- A. run-on sentence
- B. shift in voice
- C. subject-verb consistency
- D. sentence fragment

A <u>noun</u> is the name of a person, a place, a thing, or an idea.

- A **common noun** names a general or unspecific person, place, thing, or idea.

Example: A <u>spacecraft</u> entered the <u>orbit</u> of a <u>planet</u> to study its <u>rings</u> and <u>moons</u>.

- A **proper noun** names a specific person, place, or thing.

Example: A spacecraft named <u>*Cassini-Huygens*</u> entered <u>Saturn's</u> orbit to study its rings and moons.

A proper noun always begins with a capital letter.

Circle each common noun. Underline each proper noun.

1. The Eiffel Tower has more than 1,600 steps.

2. Ice worms live in glaciers in Alaska.

3. The Himalayan Mountains continue to grow because the continental plates still move.

4. In the Middle Ages, some people sold narwhal tusks as unicorn horns.

5. In Ojibwa stories, Nanabozho is the trickster hare.

6. Many parts of the Atlantic Ocean remain unexplored.

7. In 2001, a businessman named Dennis Tito became the first tourist in space.

8. Two thousand years ago, the Mayas drank hot chocolate.

9. A giant birdlike dinosaur from the late Cretaceous Period was discovered in Inner Mongolia.

10. Jackie Robinson was the first African American to play major league baseball.

Geography Factoid: Cuba is the largest island in the Greater Antilles, a chain of islands in the Caribbean Sea. Cuba is home to unique creatures. The world's smallest bird and the smallest frog both live in Cuba's thick forests.

Name _____ Date _____

A <u>noun</u> is the name of a person, a place, a thing, or an idea.

• **Concrete nouns** are nouns that you can see, touch, taste, feel, or smell.

Example: The <u>mammoth</u> was found in the <u>ice</u>.

If you forget what a concrete noun is, remember that concrete is something you can touch and see, just like you can touch both a mammoth and ice (that is, if mammoths weren't extinct).

Circle the concrete nouns in each sentence.

1. The largest hailstone was the size of a melon.

2. Lungs are made of thousands of small tubes.

3. Salt water freezes at a lower temperature than freshwater.

4. The average heart pumps 7,600 quarts (7,192 L) of blood every day.

5. The eyes of a giant squid are about the size of a human head.

6. The teeth of a beaver never stop growing.

7. Boa constrictors are excellent swimmers.

8. A tsunami wave can travel as fast as a jet airplane.

9. Dalmatians are born without spots.

10. Goose bumps on your skin help trap your body heat.

Fun Factoid: What do you do with your used chewing gum? In San Luis Obispo, California, at a special place called Bubble Gum Alley, people stick their old chewing gum on the walls. Tens of thousands of gum patties are there, and some patties are shaped into designs or pictures.

A <u>noun</u> is the name of a person, a place, a thing, or an idea.

• An **abstract noun** names a feeling, a characteristic, or an idea.

Example: The <u>beauty</u> of a rain forest can be threatened by drought.

Beauty is an abstract characteristic because you can't actually touch it.

Underline each abstract noun.

1. Intelligence can be measured by an IQ test where 100 means average intelligence.

2. *Happiness Is a Warm Puppy* is the name of a popular cartoon book by Charles Schulz.

3. Many people who exercise regularly say that they feel great contentment.

4. Which U.S. document includes the words "with liberty and justice for all"?

5. Some people still have the belief that the world is flat.

6. Many people experience fear when they speak in front of audiences.

7. A democracy is a form of government where officials are elected by the people.

8. The element carbon is known for its softness.

Science Factoid: The average human brain weighs 2.7 pounds (1,225 g). The brain's nerve cells, or neurons, send signals through a network of nerve fibers called dendrites and axons. Our memories are stored within this vast network of cells.

An appositive is a noun or pronoun.

- An **appositive** follows another noun or pronoun and identifies or explains it.
- An **appositive phrase** contains an appositive and its modifiers.

Examples: Sir Isaac Newton, <u>a famous thinker</u>, discovered the law of gravity.

Squash, <u>the oldest cultivated vegetable in North America</u>, is full of vitamins.

An appositive phrase tells the reader about the noun. Be sure to use commas around these appositive phrases. So listen to me, your friendly grammar gremlin, OK?

Circle the appositive word or phrase in each sentence. Then, draw an arrow to the noun it describes.

1. A shark's skeleton is made of cartilage, a type of elastic tissue.

2. The Burj Dubai, the world's tallest building, stands at a height of over 2,625 feet (800 m).

3. The first computer, ENIAC, was built in 1946.

4. The Milky Way, a spiral galaxy, contains stars, dust, planets, and gas.

5. Wild cats like Lusaka, a rescued lion, cannot be domesticated.

6. Half of all oxygen is produced by phytoplankton, one-celled plants on the ocean's surface.

7. Mudpuppies, types of salamanders, are also called waterdogs because of their squeaky "bark."

8. The first presidential dog to be photographed, Fido, belonged to Abraham Lincoln.

9. A serious disease once found in New Guinea, kuru, causes people to laugh uncontrollably.

10. The deepest hole ever dug, a Russian well, is about 7.5 miles (12 km) deep.

History Factoid: In 1666, Sir Isaac Newton, a mathematician, developed the theory of gravity. Some people say that Newton developed his theory when he saw an apple fall from a tree. The apple tree, a variety called Flower of Kent, became one of Britain's celebrated national treasures.

Name _____ Date _____

A plural noun refers to more than one person, place, thing, or idea.

- To make most nouns plural, add -s to the end of the word.

Examples: Bamboo plants grow faster than any other plants in the world.

Female mosquitoes bite, but male mosquitoes do not.

Some nouns that end in -o add -s to become plural, while others add -es. So, put some *potatoes* in your *kimonos*—now, that's tricky!

Write the plural form of each underlined word. Use a dictionary if you need help.

1. Most lion do not live in the jungle. _____

2. Radio rely on electromagnetic waves. _____

3. Did you know that tiger are the largest of all wildcats? _____

4. Tornado always develop from thunderstorms. _____

5. The strings of most piano have a combined pulling strength of almost 20 tons (18,144 kg). _____

6. On missions, astronauts like to eat tortilla because they do not leave crumbs. _____

7. Banjo are often used as rhythm instruments. _____

8. Spending up to 16 hours a day in the water keeps hippo cool under Africa's hot sun. _____

9. At birth, baby kangaroo are smaller than cherries. _____

10. Mount Etna, at almost 11,000 feet (3,350 m), is the highest of Europe's active volcano. _____

Science Factoid: Armadillos are the only living mammals with bony plates covering their backs, heads, tails, and legs. They dig for beetles, termites, and other insects with their long front claws.

A plural noun refers to more than one person, place, thing, or idea.

- When a noun ends in *-ch*, *-sh*, *-s*, *-x*, or *-z*, add *-es* to the end to form the plural.

- For some nouns that end in *-f* or *-fe*, change the ending to *-ves* to form the plural.

Examples: bush ⟶ bushes

            wife ⟶ wives

Some nouns that end in *-f* or *-fe* add an *-s*, such as *giraffes*, *cliffs*, and *chefs*. Spelling plural nouns right takes a little practice.

Write the plural form of each underlined word. Use a dictionary if you need help.

1. <u>Eyelash</u> help prevent dust from entering the eye. _____

2. Tennis <u>match</u> always begin with a serve from the right-hand side of the court. _____

3. Living in African deserts, fennec <u>fox</u> have hairy feet to protect them from burning in the sand. _____

4. The <u>leaf</u> of some plants trap insects for food. _____

5. The Stamp Act of 1765 was one of the first <u>tax</u> levied on American colonists. _____

6. In American colonial times, <u>church</u> were built in the center of town. _____

7. Metal lunch <u>box</u> were often decorated with pictures of TV stars. _____

8. Two <u>half</u> make a whole. _____

9. The National Museum of American History displays <u>dress</u> and jewelry worn by former first ladies. _____

10. Most chefs agree that dull <u>knife</u> are more dangerous than sharp ones.

     _____

Science Factoid: The common octopus can hide in plain sight of its predators. These octopuses quickly change skin color to match their surroundings. Hungry eels, dolphins, and sharks may swim right by.

Name _____   Date _____

A plural noun refers to more than one person, place, thing, or idea.

- When a noun ends in -y, change the -y to -i and add -es to make it plural.

Example: Honeypot ants swell up because they store nectar in their <u>bodies</u>.

But wait! If the noun ends in -ey, like *monkey*, just add an -s.

Write the plural form of each underlined word. Use a dictionary if you need help.

1. In some European <u>country</u>, people drive on the left side of the road. _____

2. Some peregrine falcons nest on skyscrapers in major <u>city</u>. _____

3. Between 1881 and 1917, Andrew Carnegie helped fund more than 2,500 <u>library</u> in the United States, Great Britain, and Canada. _____

4. <u>Mudpuppy</u> are large salamanders with bushy red gills. _____

5. Smaller than <u>pony</u>, miniature horses are about the size of large dogs and usually live 20 to 30 years. _____

6. Scientists have different <u>theory</u> about whether the universe will expand forever or begin to contract. _____

7. The United States has two major political <u>party</u>. _____

8. Warning signs for tornadoes include greenish <u>sky</u>, large hail, and a train-like roar. _____

9. A spiny lobster lays more than 700,000 eggs, but only three percent of her <u>baby</u> survive. _____

10. Monarch <u>butterfly</u> migrate up to 3,000 miles (4,828 km). _____

History Factoid: One of the stories about George Washington says that he cut down a cherry tree when he was six. He supposedly confessed by saying, "I cannot tell a lie. I did cut it with my hatchet." However, an author who wrote a book about George Washington may have made up the story. Copies of the book were first sold in 1806.

A plural noun refers to more than one person, place, thing, or idea.

• An **irregular noun** changes its spelling when it becomes plural.

Example: A saguaro <u>cactus</u> can weigh up to 10 tons (9,072 kg).

Saguaro <u>cacti</u> live about 200 years.

Most nouns are polite and act normally, but the irregular ones will try to mess you up! One *cactus*, two *cacti*— get the point?

Write the plural form of each underlined word. Use a dictionary if you need help.

1. The skin on the bottom of your two <u>foot</u> is 10 times thicker than the skin around your eyes. _____

2. Red-tailed hawks perch along roadsides to hunt <u>mouse</u>, rabbits, and other prey. _____

3. Men are much more likely to be hit by lightning than <u>woman</u>. _____

4. According to a 2008 scientific study, female <u>deer</u> are more attracted to male deer that have deep voices. _____

5. <u>Moose</u> have large hooves that act as snowshoes. _____

6. On average, ten-year-old <u>child</u> weigh more today than they did 50 years ago. _____

7. Roots, moss, and lichen are food for musk <u>ox</u> living on the Arctic tundra. _____

8. <u>Goose</u> mate with the same partner for life. _____

9. Mushrooms, molds, and puffballs are all <u>fungus</u>. _____

10. Pacu fish have humanlike <u>tooth</u>. _____

Fun Factoid: Why are shark's teeth found on most beaches? Sharks are constantly losing their teeth. And, when sharks die, their soft cartilage skeleton dissolves. Only their teeth are left. These teeth sink to the ocean floor and eventually wash to the shore.

Name _____ Date _____

A possessive noun shows ownership.

- Use -'s to show that one person, place, or thing owns something.

Example: A coconut's dried meat contains more than 60 percent oil and is used to make soap, margarine, and many other products.

Adding -'s to a regular noun won't make it plural—no how, no way! It just shows that the noun owns something.

Write the possessive form of each noun.

1. boat _____

2. alligator _____

3. principal _____

4. country _____

5. book _____

6. teacher _____

7. child _____

8. Mr. Prasad _____

9. class _____

10. turkey _____

11. Canada _____

12. media _____

Joke Break:
Riddle: Why did the bubble gum cross the road?
Answer: It was stuck on the bottom of the chicken's foot.

Name _____ Date _____

A possessive noun shows ownership.

- Use -s' to show that more than one person, place, or thing owns something.

Example: The boys' science project began to fizz when they poured vinegar on the limestone rock.

Two or more boys own the science project, so the apostrophe comes after the -s. But, be careful! An irregular noun (like *man*) is a sneaky critter! It changes its spelling when it becomes a plural possessive noun (like *men's*).

In the first column, write the plural form of each noun. Then, in the second column, write the plural possessive form of the noun.

1. elephant _____ _____

2. mouse _____ _____

3. child _____ _____

4. gorilla _____ _____

5. foot _____ _____

6. owner _____ _____

7. president _____ _____

8. leaf _____ _____

9. woman _____ _____

10. sheep _____ _____

Fun Factoid: Birds poop everywhere! This is one reason why most people do not let their pet birds fly freely around their homes. However, some companies are trying to change that. They make diapers for birds. The diapers collect the birds' droppings and come in multiple sizes.

Name _____ Date _____

A complete sentence always has a <u>verb</u>.

- An **action verb** tells what someone or something is doing.

Example: Many insects <u>breathe</u> through holes along the sides of their bodies.

Breathe in … breathe out. The word *breathe* is an action word, so it's a verb!

Circle the verb in each sentence.

1. Starfish eat clams.

2. Food rots because of bacteria or fungi.

3. The Pinyin Chinese language forms words with about 20,000 characters.

4. Pythons live in southern Asia, Africa, and Australia.

5. Gases in your stomach create a rumbling sound.

6. Macaws crack nuts with their powerful beaks.

7. Komodo dragons eat about 80 percent of their body weight in one meal.

8. King Tutankhamun's tomb contained many Egyptian treasures.

9. A man from Nepal climbed Mount Everest a record 19 times.

10. Food usually passes through a person's body in two to three days.

Science Factoid: A person sometimes feels a sharp pain in the side of his body if he exercises immediately after he eats. One theory suggests that because the stomach becomes heavier after a person eats, it then pulls on the ligaments that hold it in place. If exercise involves bouncing up and down, the stomach strains the ligaments.

A present-tense verb expresses action that is happening now.

- **Present-tense verbs** can express action or state of being.

Examples: About 8 million bolts of lightning strike Earth each day.

Hainan black-crested gibbons are among the most critically endangered primates in the world.

When do the bolts of lightning strike? Now! When are those gibbons endangered? Now! So, these verbs are in the present tense.

Underline each present-tense verb.

1. An asteroid belt lies between the orbits of Mars and Jupiter.

2. People dream during 25 percent of their sleep time.

3. Lungs take oxygen from the air and remove carbon dioxide from the body.

4. Aquatic shrews run on the surface of water.

5. Orangutans build large platform-like nests from branches and leaves.

6. The highest tides in the world occur in the Bay of Fundy in Canada.

7. A person's small intestine measures about 20 feet (6 m) long.

8. More people speak Mandarin Chinese and English than any other languages.

9. The world's largest flower grows to 3 feet (91 cm) wide and weighs up to 24 pounds (11 kg).

10. About 1.5 million people live in the Arctic.

Science Factoid: Everybody exhibits a different physical appearance on the outside. People differ inside their bodies too. People's internal organs, such as their hearts, livers, and kidneys, vary in size, shape, and sometimes location.

A past-tense verb expresses action that happened in the past.

- Most **past-tense verbs** are formed by adding -ed to the end of a present-tense verb.
- An **irregular verb** changes its spelling in the past tense.

The regular verb in number 4 has a short vowel followed by a consonant. So, double the last consonant and add -ed. Tricky!

Examples: In 1578, Sir Francis Drake sailed through the Strait of Magellan.

A pot-bellied pig broke a record for the highest jump by a pig.

Write the past tense of each underlined word. Use a dictionary if you need help.

1. Thomas Edison patent 1,093 inventions. _____

2. In 1895, Joshua Slocum begin the first solo voyage around the world in a small sailboat. _____

3. In 1867, the United States buy Alaska from Russia for 7.2 million dollars. _____

4. Native Americans pop corn thousands of years ago. _____

5. U.S. President Zachary Taylor bring his horse to the White House and let it graze on the lawn. _____

6. The largest diamond weigh 1.4 pounds (621 g). _____

7. The shortest American president stand 5 feet 4 inches (162.56 cm) tall. _____

8. Ancient Egyptians use umbrellas for protection from the sun. _____

9. Louis Pasteur develop pasteurization, which kills harmful bacteria in milk. _____

10. Abraham Lincoln grow a beard shortly after he won the presidency. _____

A future-tense verb expresses action that will happen in the future.

- A **future-tense verb** is formed by placing the helping verb *will* in front of the present-tense verb.

Examples: My metal detector <u>will find</u> coins buried 12 inches (30 cm) deep.

<u>Will</u> you <u>explain</u> why men are color-blind more often than women?

Uh-oh! The second example is a question. That's why the helping verb *will* is separated from the main verb *explain*.

Underline the complete future-tense verb in each sentence.

1. A tree will create sticky resin, or sap, to seal any wounds in its bark.

2. Adding dandelion leaves to a salad will boost its vitamins A and C.

3. Many desert animals will hunt only after the sun sets.

4. If you do not plant grass on a sand dune, the sand will erode.

5. Brightly colored and fragrant flowers will attract insects.

6. The jackfruit tree's fruit will grow to weigh as much as 60 pounds (27 kg).

7. During autumn, leaves will lose their chlorophyll and change colors.

8. Contracting the diaphragm's muscles will expand the lungs, which draws in air.

9. The structure of your brain will change every time you have a new thought or memory.

10. A bee colony will make between 20,000 and 40,000 separate trips to collect enough nectar to make just 1 pound (454 g) of honey.

Science Factoid: Often, coconut palm trees will grow near the sea. When the coconuts are ripe, they will fall to the ground and roll into the ocean. Coconuts will float for many months in the ocean until they reach an island. Then, the coconuts will germinate and grow into new trees.

A <u>helping verb</u> helps the main verb express its tense.

- When most main verbs use the helping verbs *have*, *has*, or *had*, the main verb adds *-ed* to the end. This is called the **past participle**.
- **Irregular verbs** change their spelling when they are used as past participles.

Example: Often, supercell thunderstorms <u>have</u> <u>produced</u> the most destructive tornadoes.

> If you don't know the past participle of a verb, use your dictionary. It will show you the past and past participle forms next to the verb.

Write the past participle of each word in parentheses.

1. In 400 BC, Chinese inventors had (fly) _____ kites to test weather conditions.

2. Most lightning deaths have (occur) _____ between June and August.

3. My friend from Asia has (eat) _____ roasted giant water bugs.

4. Goliath tigerfish have (devour) _____ small crocodiles.

5. Scientists had (think) _____ that coelacanth fish became extinct millions of years ago.

6. Eagles have (build) _____ large nests called aeries in tall treetops.

7. Common wood frogs have (freeze) _____ in winter but thawed in spring.

8. The female anglerfish has (catch) _____ many smaller fish using a lure, which looks like a fishing pole.

9. Hailstones have (fall) _____ at more than 100 miles (161 km) per hour.

10. Until we studied the campfire handbook, we had not (know) _____ that redwood bark is fire resistant.

A verb in the <u>subjunctive mood</u> shows a wish or an unreal situation.

- A phrase such as *I wish that* uses the verb form *were* instead of *was*.
- A phrase such as *I would…if* uses the verb form *were* instead of *was*.

Examples: <u>I wish that</u> I **were** immune to the common cold.

<u>I would</u> never catch a cold again if I **were** immune to them.

Here's a hot tip! Look at number 5. Use *were* when a phrase begins with *as if* or *as though*.

Circle each correct verb in parentheses.

1. I wish that I (was, were) going to Greece so that I could see the Parthenon.

2. I could not see the difference between red and green if I (was, were) color-blind.

3. I wish that I (was, were) an entomologist because I love to study insects.

4. If the wind (was, were) to blow faster, the temperature would feel colder.

5. Mahatma Gandhi said, "Learn as if you (was, were) to live forever."

6. If it (was, were) raining today, you would see many earthworms on the sidewalk.

7. If Carla (was, were) an expert on sea horses, she would know that the male sea horse gives birth to its young.

8. If I (was, were) a spittlebug, I could jump 100 times my length.

9. Arianna's throat was inflamed as if she (was, were) exposed to strep throat bacteria.

10. Some people mistakenly believe that if a person (was, were) to hold a toad, the toad would give the person warts.

Fun Factoid: Jim Smith is a rather common name in North America. However, if your name were Jim Smith, you could belong to the Jim Smith Society. Only people named Jim Smith are allowed to join this club. Members of the club come from all over to celebrate together. Now, don't you wish that your name were Jim Smith?

Review: Nouns and Verbs

Underline each noun and circle each verb.

1. An octopus has three hearts.

2. Some spiders rub the hairs on their legs together to make a hissing noise.

3. In 2008, scientists in Madagascar discovered the fossil of a beach-ball-sized amphibian.

4. Baby elephants, or calves, weigh about 200 pounds (91 kg) at birth.

5. One day on Venus equals about 243 days on Earth.

6. In the original story from France, Cinderella wears fur slippers.

7. Nyctophobia is the fear of darkness.

8. In the United States, about 86 percent of plastic water bottles become litter or garbage.

9. In the original movie, King Kong was an 18-inch puppet.

10. Jackrabbits eat juicy plants like cacti.

11. Some swans carry their babies on their backs across the water.

12. The tree snake glides from tree to tree.

History Factoid: Mark Twain, the famous writer, was born when Halley's comet appeared in the sky. When the comet returned 75 years later, Mark Twain passed away.

An <u>adjective</u> is a word that describes a noun or a pronoun.

- An **adjective** can come before or after the word it describes.

Examples: Rainwater is <u>acidic</u>.
Acidic rainwater can dissolve rocks.

Adjectives can tell what kind, which one, or how many. They're called descriptive adjectives. Wait a minute! Isn't *descriptive* a descriptive adjective? Ha!

Underline each adjective.

1. A healthy person should walk about 10,000 steps every day.

2. Mosses grow in cool, moist environments.

3. Canada is a constitutional monarchy, which is ruled by the Queen of England.

4. President Abraham Lincoln was a tall man who often wore a top hat.

5. The upper jaw of a sailfish looks like a spear.

6. One person's two feet can differ in size and shape.

7. Koalas survive best in wide spaces with about 100 eucalyptus trees.

8. Cinnamon, a common baking spice, comes from the inner bark of a small evergreen tree.

9. In the Nazca Desert, people skillfully created huge pictures of animals and people on the ground.

10. In the 1930s, farm women often made dresses and curtains from feed sacks and flour bags.

History Factoid: Canada did not have a national flag until February 15, 1965. Before 1965, the Canadian Red Ensign was used. Now, the maple leaf flies above Parliament Hill.

Name _____ Date _____

An <u>adjective</u> is a word that describes a noun or a pronoun.

• A **proper adjective** is an adjective formed from a proper noun.

Example: Dr. Ashley Strope was the first woman to drive a <u>Mars</u> rover.

Don't be tricked by number 8! *White House* is the complete name of the building, so it's a proper noun.

Circle each proper adjective.

1. In Cherokee myth, Nunhyunuwi is a dangerous, man-eating giant.

2. The tulip is named after the Persian word for *turban*.

3. The Enigma was a German invention used to send secret messages during World War II.

4. The medical symbol that shows two snakes comes from an ancient Greek legend.

5. Viking ships could carry 100 men.

6. Mayan Indians decorated their teeth with fabulous jewels.

7. The first five-cent U.S. postage stamp pictured Benjamin Franklin.

8. When the French ambassador visited Theodore Roosevelt at the White House, the president's dog tore the visitor's pants.

9. About 400 to 500 Siberian tigers live in the wild.

10. The Canadian coastline, which is 151,019 miles (243,042 km) long, is the longest in the world.

Sports Factoid: The game of hockey may be based on several British field sports. The French also played a game with hooked sticks. People must have tried playing these games on ice. This variation caught on during long Canadian winters and spread into Scandinavian countries and Russia.

An <u>adjective</u> is a word that describes a noun or a pronoun.

- The words *a*, *an*, and *the* are **limiting adjectives**. They also are called **articles**.

Example: In 1869, <u>the</u> Wyoming territorial legislature gave women <u>the</u> right to vote, which remained <u>the</u> law even after <u>the</u> territory became <u>a</u> state in 1890.

Just like we have speed limits, nouns need limits too! A limiting adjective comes before the noun. It shows whether something is definite (*the*) or indefinite (*a* or *an*).

Circle each limiting adjective.

1. The flag of Denmark is considered one of the oldest national flags in the world.

2. The national flag of Afghanistan has undergone more changes in the twentieth century than any other country's flag.

3. A red maple leaf, a Canadian symbol, is at the center of Canada's flag.

4. The 13 stripes on an American flag represent the original 13 colonies.

5. The red color of the cross on the flag of Iceland symbolizes the island's volcanic fires.

6. The American Red Cross flag is the reverse of the red and white flag of Switzerland.

7. The American flag has a white star to represent each of the country's 50 states.

8. The flag of Chile uses white to symbolize the snowy mountains of the Andes.

9. The Japanese flag displays a red dot to represent the sun without its rays.

10. The unique shape of Nepal's flag is a combination of two red pennants.

History Factoid: A pledge to the U.S. flag was first published in 1892. Over the years, the pledge has undergone several changes in wording. In 1954, a law stated that a citizen should stand and place the right hand over the heart while reciting the pledge. However, the U.S. Supreme Court has since ruled that people cannot be required to recite the Pledge of Allegiance.

Name _____ Date _____

An <u>adjective</u> can compare nouns.

- **Comparative adjectives** compare two things. Most comparative adjectives are formed by adding -*er* to the end of the adjective.

Examples: A quark is <u>smaller</u> than an electron.

Gila monsters are <u>more dangerous</u> than any other lizard.

Look at number 3. Adjectives with three or more syllables use *more* in front of them. They don't add -*er* to the end. Some two-syllable adjectives use *more* too—and I couldn't be *more certain*!

Write the comparative form of each adjective in parentheses.

1. Some mountains on Mars are much (tall) _____ than Mount Everest.

2. One species of Ecuadorian ant is (tricky) _____ to see than other species because the tiny ants cover themselves with mud and move extremely slowly.

3. The eyesight of the mantis shrimp is (amazing) _____ than that of other species of shrimp because of its ability to see 12 or 13 primary colors.

4. Helium balloons float because helium is (light) _____ than air.

5. Transistors were (sturdy) _____ than the vacuum tubes they replaced.

6. Garden spiders are generally (colorful) _____ than house spiders.

7. Some people may think that roasted grubs are (tasty) _____ than chocolate-covered ants.

8. About 4 million years ago, some South American rodents weighed 2,200 pounds (998 kg) and were (immense) _____ than cows.

9. Famous for its wet weather, the city of Vancouver is even (rainy) _____ than Seattle.

10. In the English language, the letter *T* is (popular) _____ than the letter *S*.

Name _____ Date _____

An <u>adjective</u> can compare nouns.

- **Superlative adjectives** compare three or more things. Most superlative adjectives are formed by adding -*est* to the end of the adjective.

Beware! Superlative adjectives can be tricky. Some longer adjectives use *most* in front of them. They don't add -*est* to the end.

Examples: Platinum is the third <u>heaviest</u> element after iridium and osmium.

Desert locusts are the <u>most destructive</u> insects on Earth.

Write the superlative form of each adjective in parentheses.

1. Composed primarily of ice crystals, cirrus clouds are among the (high) _____ clouds.

2. The (hot) _____ temperature ever recorded on Earth was 136°F (57.8°C) in Libya.

3. With many traits of its wild ancestors, the cat is the (new) _____ domesticated animal.

4. Most often, the (hungry) _____ animals, such as the shrew and the hummingbird, are also the smallest animals.

5. The (common) _____ blood type is O positive.

6. Australia's Great Barrier Reef is called the (large) _____ living organism in the world.

7. The (expensive) _____ ice-cream sundae in the world costs $1,000 and is topped with 23-carat, edible gold.

8. Orangutans are some of the (solitary) _____ mammals because they do not live in social groups.

9. In the rain forest, ants are the (numerous) _____ species.

10. Built in 1889, the Eiffel Tower is one of Europe's (famous) _____ landmarks.

Name _____ Date _____

An <u>adverb</u> is a word that describes a verb, an adjective, or another adverb.

- An **adverb** can tell *how*.

Example: In the early 1900s, the botanist George Washington Carver <u>thoroughly</u> researched peanut cultivation.

Ask yourself, "How did George Washington Carver research peanut cultivation?" He researched it *thoroughly*. So, *thoroughly* is an adverb. (It's OK to talk to yourself during grammar time!)

- An adverb can tell *where* or *in which direction*.

Example: Because of its volcanic activity, visitors to White Island, New Zealand, wear gas masks when they get <u>there</u>.

Underline each adverb.

1. In Jamaica, bands seem to play lively music everywhere.

2. Neil Armstrong took the first step on the moon while the world watched below.

3. Beekeepers must remove honeycombs carefully to avoid hurting the bees.

4. When a young kangaroo feels threatened, he quickly dives for his mother's pouch.

5. In the last 50 years, Sicily's volcano, Mount Etna, has been increasingly active.

6. Brain activity gradually slows down as we move through the first stages of sleep.

7. Are you quite certain that the national bird of India is the peacock?

8. In China, a person's last name appears first.

9. A batting helmet can protect a baseball player if a ball accidentally hits him in the head.

10. The outermost layer of skin, or epidermis, grows outward as older cells die and flake off.

Science Factoid: Contrary to popular belief, lemmings do not jump off cliffs voluntarily. These small rodents may slip off a ledge accidentally or occasionally when they swim in search of food, but they do not willingly hurl themselves by the hundreds off cliffs.

Name _____ Date _____

An <u>adverb</u> is a word that describes a verb, an adjective, or another adverb.

- An **adverb** can tell *when*.

Example: <u>Daily</u>, the tide rises and falls.

An adverb can appear just about anywhere in a sentence. You could also write *The tide rises and falls daily*, or even, *The tide daily rises and falls*. Mix it up, and it still works!

Underline the adverbs that tell *when* in each sentence.

1. The British once ruled India.

2. Usually, the human brain's short-term memory can hold seven to 10 digits, or units, of information.

3. Recently, there was a trend among homeowners to hang Christmas trees upside down.

4. Snakes never eat plants.

5. Flamingoes sometimes sleep standing on one leg.

6. Molds often grow on dairy products, bread, and jellies.

7. The blue whales' cries can travel hundreds of miles underwater, but the whales frequently make sounds that humans cannot hear.

8. Normally, babies can recognize their parents' faces about three months after birth.

9. A large swarm of locusts can consume 423 million pounds (192 million kg) of vegetation daily.

10. Tomorrow, we will learn about the Mariana Trench, which at 35,810 feet (10,915 m) is the deepest part of the ocean.

Science Factoid: Bath towels are often made of cotton because this material can absorb 25 times its own weight in water. Towels are usually made with looped strands of cotton because the small loops act like sponges.

An <u>adverb</u> can compare actions.

- Use a **comparative adverb** to compare two actions. Add -er to the end or add *more* in front of an adverb to form the comparative.

Examples: The killer whale swam <u>faster</u> than the bottlenose dolphin.

The killer whale swam <u>more quickly</u> than the bottlenose dolphin.

- Use a **superlative adverb** to compare the actions of three or more nouns or pronouns. Add -est to the end or add *most* in front of an adverb to form the superlative.

Examples: Of all birds, the peregrine falcon flies the <u>fastest</u>.

Of all birds, the peregrine falcon flies the <u>most quickly</u>.

Look at number 6. *Well* is an irregular adverb. It does not use -er, -est, *more*, or *most*. The comparative form of *well* is *better*. The superlative form of *well* is *best*. This is one you just have to memorize!

Write either the comparative or the superlative form of each adverb in parentheses.

1. Traveling at 0.15 miles (0.24 km) per hour, the three-toed sloth moves (slowly) _____ of all mammals.

2. After Yukon gold was discovered in 1896, the United States' purchase of Alaska was accepted (enthusiastically) _____ than in 1867.

3. Many prehistoric species may have disappeared (suddenly) _____ during years with volcanic eruptions than during quieter years.

4. During summer, the sun in Antarctica can burn the skin (severely) _____ than in the United States.

5. The bright green chlorophyll in leaves absorbs sunlight (efficiently) _____ than the yellow pigmented carotene.

6. Cinderella May, a dog that set a world record when it leaped 68 inches (172.7 cm) in the air, jumped (well) _____ than my dog.

7. The sperm whale dives (deep) _____ than other toothed whales.

Name _____ Date _____

Review: Adjectives and Adverbs

Circle each correct word choice in parentheses.

1. Mr. Garcia's students were (most interested, interestedest) in learning about early English explorers.

2. The class assumed (correct, correctly) that Columbus was not the first European to discover America.

3. They (certain, certainly) knew that Leif Eriksson, a Viking, was the first European to reach North America's mainland.

4. They agreed that Eriksson must have been (brave, bravely) to cross the ocean in his longboat.

5. The students (accurate, accurately) remembered that Leif Eriksson landed in the New World in about AD 1000.

6. Mr. Garcia explained that England had claimed that John Cabot was the (most early, earliest) to land in the New World in 1497.

7. Cabot was actually Italian, but he is (more commonly, commonlier) known as an English explorer.

8. This was the reason that England (bold, boldly) claimed to own the entire east coast of North America.

9. Sir Francis Drake was another explorer who did (good, well) for England.

10. Drake was the first Englishman to sail (successful, successfully) around the world.

11. Mr. Garcia's class felt (bad, badly) to learn that the English navigator Henry Hudson died at sea.

12. Hudson had been (unsuccessful, unsuccessfully) at finding a northwest passage from the Arctic to the Far East.

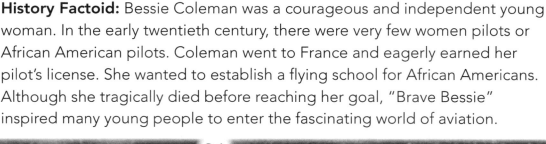

History Factoid: Bessie Coleman was a courageous and independent young woman. In the early twentieth century, there were very few women pilots or African American pilots. Coleman went to France and eagerly earned her pilot's license. She wanted to establish a flying school for African Americans. Although she tragically died before reaching her goal, "Brave Bessie" inspired many young people to enter the fascinating world of aviation.

Name _____ Date _____

A **pronoun** is a word that takes the place of a noun.

- A **subject pronoun** does the action. Subject pronouns include: *I, you, he, she, it, we,* and *they.*
- An **object pronoun** receives the verb's action. Object pronouns include: *me, you, him, her, it, us,* and *them.*

subject
pronoun ⌐   ⌐ verb
Examples: I heard the barking dog.

The barking dog heard me.
     verb ⌐   ⌐ object
          pronoun

A subject pronoun, like *I*, is usually before the verb. An object pronoun, like *me*, is usually after the verb. Where it is tells you what it is!

Underline each correct pronoun in parentheses.

1. A science teacher told (I, me) that the world's smallest mammal is the bumblebee bat.

2. Adam and (I, me) noticed that the nonpoisonous milk snake looks a lot like the deadly coral snake.

3. Claire explained to (I, me) how the gravitational pull of the moon affects Earth's tides.

4. Kami and (I, me) read that chimpanzees use sticks and rocks for tools.

5. When Dad first showed (I, me) this tortoise, she was only the size of quarter.

6. My parents want (I, me) to eat spinach because it is high in vitamin K.

7. My brother and (I, me) learned that macaw birds can live to be 60 years old.

8. (I, Me) know that sunspots are islands of magnetism that may explode into solar flares.

9. After Mom and (I, me) scared the opossum, he played dead for six hours.

10. The eel's slippery slime layer surprised Cameron and (I, me).

Joke Break:
Student: "Miss Grundy, someone called me a storyteller."
Miss Grundy: "I can't believe that!"

A pronoun is a word that takes the place of a noun.

- A **subject pronoun** does the action. Subject pronouns include: *I, you, he, she, it, we,* and *they.*
- An **object pronoun** receives the verb's action. Object pronouns include: *me, you, him, her, it, us,* and *them.*

A subject pronoun, such as *he* or *she,* is usually before the verb. An object pronoun, such as *him* or *her,* is usually after the verb.

Example: She passed the jumping beans ——— subject pronouns

quickly to him. She learned that

larvae were inside them. ——— object pronouns

Circle each correct pronoun in parentheses.

1. When will Mr. Chu and (he, him) explore the volcanic island of Krakatau?

2. I told (she, her) that the eye's iris is really a muscle that controls the size of the pupil.

3. In Captain John Smith's personal accounts, Pocahontas supposedly rescued (he, him).

4. The professor informed Michael and (she, her) that the tallest peaks of the Himalayas are always covered in snow.

5. When (she, her) and I read that rabbits and hares were not the same animal, we were amazed.

6. (He, Him) and I are surprised that four of the first five U.S. presidents were from Virginia.

7. (He, Him) and David read that about 1.5 million species of insects have been identified.

8. Tell (she, her) when Thomas Edison produced the first movie film with his kinetoscope.

9. Ms. Avery showed (he, him) that dikes were formed from magma millions of years ago.

10. I asked (she, her) why some plants and animals on the Galapagos Islands are not found anywhere else on Earth.

Name _____ Date _____

A <u>pronoun</u> is a word that takes the place of a noun.

- A **subject pronoun** does the action. Subject pronouns include: *I, you, he, she, it, we,* and *they.*
- An **object pronoun** receives the verb's action. Object pronouns include: *me, you, him, her, it, us,* and *them.*

It can be either a subject pronoun or an object pronoun. *It* doesn't change form or spelling! So, you better get *it* before *it* gets you, get it?

Example: <u>John Davis</u> was the first person to set foot on the <u>continent of Antarctica</u>.

↓

He was the first person to set foot on <u>it</u>. ← —————— object pronoun

————— subject pronoun

Rewrite each sentence, replacing each set of underlined words with the correct subject or object pronoun.

1. <u>Honeybees</u> dance to tell other bees where to find <u>food</u>. _____

   _____

2. <u>Many cities</u> add <u>fluoride</u> to drinking water to strengthen children's teeth. _____

   _____

3. <u>Star-nosed moles</u> can identify and eat <u>their food</u> in about 250 milliseconds. _____

   _____

4. <u>Small frogs</u> rained down in a Serbian town, which made <u>villagers</u> run for cover. _____

   _____

5. <u>The forest ranger</u> showed <u>my sister and me</u> redwood trees that were 2,000 years old.

   _____

6. In South America, <u>people</u> smoke tarantulas over a fire before eating <u>the spiders</u>. _____

   _____

Science Factoid: Each day, your nose and sinuses make more than 1/2 cup (125 mL) of mucus. Mucus is the slimy, sticky stuff inside your nose. It traps dust, germs, and pollen and keeps them from entering your lungs. If your lungs get irritated, they could become infected. Mucus helps keep you healthy!

A possessive pronoun shows ownership of something. It takes the place of a possessive noun.

- **Pronouns** that show ownership include *my, mine, your, yours, his, her, hers, its, our, ours, their,* or *theirs.*

Examples: Because I am an adult and you are a child, <u>my</u> fingernails do not grow as quickly as <u>your</u> fingernails.

Because I am an adult and you are a child, <u>mine</u> do not grow as quickly as <u>yours</u>.

The second example uses *yours. Yours* refers to *your fingernails,* but the noun *fingernails* is missing. Use *yours, mine, ours, theirs,* or *hers* in such cases. But, you better not add an apostrophe. If you do, it's not my fault—it's *yours!*

Circle each correct pronoun in parentheses.

1. The skin on (our, ours) lips, the palms of (our, ours) hands, and the soles of (our, ours) feet do not have hair.

2. People have about the same number of hairs on (their, theirs) bodies as other primates.

3. The hair on (your, yours) body is much shorter and finer than a chimpanzee's hair.

4. Eyebrows are one of (our, ours) most distinctive and expressive facial features.

5. (Their, theirs) eyebrows protect (their, theirs) eyes from sweat dripping down (their, theirs) foreheads.

6. Every hair on my body and (your, yours) contains dead cells.

7. That is why we do not feel pain when someone cuts (our, ours) hair.

8. (Her, hers) hair is shiny because an oil gland is attached to each hair root, or follicle.

9. On average, a person has more than 100,000 hairs on (his, their) head but loses about 100 hairs every day.

Name _____ Date _____

A demonstrative pronoun refers to a specific person or object and agrees in number.

- *This* and *these* refer to objects that are near.
- *That* and *those* refer to objects that are far away.

Examples: (Those) are whale <u>sharks</u>, which are the
largest fish in the sea. (far away)

(This) is a whale <u>shark</u> in the picture. (near)

Look out, though, because *that* can act like an adjective too, such as in this example: *That* shark is all that! (*That* describes the shark.)

Circle each demonstrative pronoun. Then, underline the noun it refers to.

1. That is the lobster that took seven years to gain 1 pound (0.45 kg).

2. These are hummingbirds, which can fly backward.

3. These are the 33 desert islands that form the country of Bahrain.

4. These are coprolites, which are fossilized dinosaur droppings.

5. Those are poisonous dart frogs, which are brightly colored to warn predators.

6. That is an Asian elephant, because it has smaller ears than an African elephant.

7. This is a one-year-old eel, which is called an elver.

8. This is Big Ben, the famous clock tower with four clock faces, each 23 feet (7 m) across.

9. That is a chirping sound coming from the hummingbird's unusual tail feathers, not from its throat.

Geography Factoid: Tropical rain forests are known for receiving vast amounts of rain. These heavy rains dissolve nutrients in the soil. This is what makes the top layers of soil relatively infertile. That then causes the trees to have wide but shallow roots. This creates unstable rain forest trees because their roots are not strong anchors in the ground.

Review: Pronouns

Circle each correct pronoun in parentheses.

1. Tell (he, him) that rats were once one of human's worst enemies because they carried diseases and destroyed food.

2. Doug and (me, I) learned that some cicada nymphs stay underground for years living on the liquid in plant roots.

3. An archerfish can spit water like a blowgun at land insects to catch (them, they).

4. Some scientists have tried to determine the population of tigers in India by counting (their, theirs) pugmarks, or paw prints.

5. The frogfish has leglike fins and uses (they, them) to bounce on the ocean floor.

6. When the leafy sea dragon swam by (her, she), she thought it was just a piece of seaweed.

7. The barreleye fish has a transparent head, which (we, us) think looks disgusting.

8. A termite may secrete a sticky substance at (it's, its) enemy to protect (it's, its) colony.

9. Pet tarantulas like (your, yours) may look creepy with their hairy bodies and legs, but they are harmless to humans.

10. (Us, We) were surprised to learn that the African lungfish can survive for months out of water.

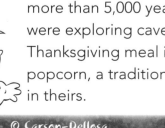

History Factoid: You may not realize that popcorn has been around for more than 5,000 years. Scientists discovered popped corn while they were exploring caves in New Mexico. It was also probably part of the first Thanksgiving meal in Massachusetts. Today, some of us enjoy flavored popcorn, a tradition of Native Americans who used dried herbs and spices in theirs.

Name _____ Date _____

A preposition is a word that relates a noun or pronoun to other words in the sentence.

- Common prepositions include: *about, across, after, around, at, behind, by, during, for, from, in, of, through, toward, under, upon,* and *with*.

Example: A sheet <u>of</u> graphene is nearly as thick as one atom.

The word of is a preposition. It shows how the words *sheet* and *graphene* are connected.

Circle each preposition.

1. Graphene is the thinnest material in the world.

2. About 25,000 sheets of graphene are equivalent in height to one sheet of regular paper.

3. Graphene is made of carbon, one of the most common elements in the world.

4. Graphene is produced mainly for use in electronic devices.

5. In 2008, graphene was used in the production of the world's smallest transistor.

6. Transistors control the electricity that passes through them.

7. Over the next several years, graphene transistors might replace silicon chips.

8. Scientists look toward a future where electronic devices with graphene transistors will be even smaller.

9. In terms of mass, graphene is the most expensive material on Earth.

10. A tiny piece of graphene as thick as a human hair could cost more than $1,500.

History Factoid: Before the 1947 invention of transistors, people depended on vacuum tubes for electronic devices. But, vacuum tubes were large, expensive, inefficient, and easily broken. The size of vacuum tubes meant that electronic devices were also very large. Transistors helped electronic devices become smaller and faster. Then, the microchip, which is about the size of a grain of rice, was invented and the rest is history!

Name _____ Date _____

A preposition is a word that relates a noun or pronoun to other words in the sentence.

- Use the preposition *between* when the object of the preposition is two people or things.
- Use the preposition *among* when the object of the preposition is three or more people or things.

A *troop of baboons* must be a lot! So, *among* is definitely the right preposition to use.

Examples: The difference <u>between</u> a vertebrate and an invertebrate is that a vertebrate has a spinal column.

The troop of baboons chattered <u>among</u> themselves as they groomed each other to remove insects and dead skin.

Circle each correct preposition in parentheses.

1. (Among, Between) all of the known species of spiders, only about 25 have venom that affects humans.

2. One difference (between, among) a real diamond and the synthetic diamond cubic zirconia is that a real diamond is harder.

3. The space (among, between) your brain and your skull is filled with a protective clear, colorless fluid.

4. In a race (between, among) a good human swimmer and an eel, the human would win.

5. In 2004, the *Cassini* spacecraft flew (among, between) the many rings of Saturn.

6. The small intestine is located (among, between) the stomach and the large intestine.

7. (Among, Between) all breeds of dogs, only 11 are generally recommended for people with allergies.

Science Factoid: In 1958, a squirrel monkey named Gordo was placed in a Jupiter rocket and launched into outer space between Earth and the moon. Gordo survived the blastoff, the 600-mile (966-kilometer) flight, and the splashdown in the Atlantic Ocean. Gordo is among a handful of animals that have helped humankind travel into space.

Name _____ Date _____

A prepositional phrase is a group of words that begins with a preposition.

- A **prepositional phrase** ends with a noun or pronoun called the **object of the preposition**.

Example: I looked up at the thin, cirrus clouds and realized that the weather would probably change.

object of the preposition

It's time to talk to yourself! Look at the example and ask yourself, "At what?" The answer is "at the *clouds*," so *clouds* is the object of the preposition. It's the noun or pronoun that the preposition refers to.

Underline each prepositional phrase. Then, circle each object of the preposition.

1. Oarfish, one of the longest fish in the sea, live deep below the surface.

2. The chemical symbol for gold is Au, which is short for the Latin *aurum*.

3. The mercury barometer, invented by Evangelista Torricelli, measures air pressure.

4. In 1937, Amelia Earhart's plane vanished over the Pacific Ocean.

5. Fog forms when water vapor condenses on dust in the atmosphere.

6. After 365 days, 6 hours, 9 minutes, and 9.54 seconds, Earth completes its orbit around the sun.

7. Tundra ecosystems are found in the Arctic and on mountaintops where it is cold, windy, and dry.

8. Hundreds of unusual mummies have been found in the bogs of Ireland, Denmark, and other European countries.

9. In the winter, the highway department spreads salt on icy roads.

10. Jesse Owens broke three world records and won four gold medals at the 1936 Olympic Games in Berlin, Germany.

Science Factoid: Nature has its own form of fireworks. Every July and August, Earth drifts through a trail of dust scattered by the Comet Swift-Tuttle. Known as the Perseid meteor shower, dozens of shooting stars per hour bombard Earth's atmosphere as the comet's debris comes into contact with Earth's atmosphere.

A <u>conjunction</u> is a word that joins words or groups of words.

- **Coordinating conjunctions** combine related sentences. Common coordinating conjunctions include the words *or, and, but,* and *so.*

Examples: Seaweed is slimy, <u>but</u> it is very nutritious, containing iodine and vitamin C.

I visited Japan, <u>and</u> I tried to eat sushi wrapped in seaweed there.

Some people dry seaweed in the sun <u>or</u> crisp it over an open flame.

Some seaweed is not edible, <u>so</u> know your seaweed!

No *ifs, ands,* or *buts* about it! You need to know the right conjunction to use. *But* shows contrast. *And* joins similar ideas. *Or* shows a choice. *So* shows that the second idea is the result of the first idea.

Circle the best coordinating conjunction for each sentence.

1. Potatoes are a form of complex carbohydrate, (but, or, so) they are a good source of energy for athletes.

2. Throughout the world, people eat white or Irish potatoes as a staple food, (and, or, but) potatoes are also sometimes fed to livestock.

3. Potatoes are a cool-weather crop, (so, but, or) they grow best in areas with cool summers.

4. As a potato grows, it develops "eyes," (or, but, and) these can be cut out and planted to grow new potatoes.

5. Potatoes can be grown from the pieces with "eyes," (and, or, so) they can be grown from whole potatoes.

6. Sometimes, small clusters of berries will grow on the tops of potato plants, (or, and, so) they look like little green cherry tomatoes.

7. Inside the berries are potato seeds, (or, and, but) they can be taken out and planted.

8. Potato berries are not edible, (but, and, so) many types of berries are.

A conjunction is a word that joins words or groups of words.

- **Correlative conjunctions** join two equal parts of a sentence and are always used in pairs. These include *either … or, both … and, neither … nor,* and *not only … but (also).*

Example: Slugs can be <u>either</u> land-dwelling <u>or</u> sea-dwelling.

Either you get this rule *or* you don't! Correlative conjunctions always come in pairs. You can't have one without the other!

Write the correct correlative conjunction for each sentence.

1. Slugs not only eat your flowers, _____ they also leave slimy trails on your patio.

2. Neither a land slug _____ a sea slug moves quickly when pulling itself along on a single foot.

3. Slugs can be herbivores or carnivores, either eating leafy plants _____ devouring earthworms and insects.

4. The ghost slug's origin is a mystery, but both its lack of eyes _____ its pale color means it may have evolved underground.

5. When threatened by a lobster, one sea slug produces not only ink _____ the chemical opaline to blast at the predator.

6. Unlike other mollusks, a slug either has no shell _____ it has a partial shell under its skin.

7. Sea slugs either crawl on the bottom of the ocean _____ they swim in graceful, winding movements.

8. Some sea slugs can avoid their enemies either by swimming away _____ by releasing a foul smell.

Science Factoid: A nudibranch is a type of sea slug. It not only breathes through gills that stick out of its back, but it also can pull the gills inside its body when attacked. Nudibranchs can live in both the most frigid sea and the warmest tropical ocean. A nudibranch can be either long and thin or chubby and round. Because a nudibranch has neither a nose nor a tongue, it uses its tentacles to smell and taste.

A **conjunction** is a word that joins words or groups of words.

- A **subordinating conjunction** begins a dependent clause. Common subordinating conjunctions include *although, while, because, if, so, when,* and *since.*

      dependent clause

Example: | Although a tarantula's bite is painful, | its venom is weaker than the venom of a typical bee.

A dependent clause is weak and needy! *Although a tarantula's bite is painful* just can't stand alone. It needs the main part of this sentence about the *venom.* Now, that's a strong, independent clause! The subordinating conjunction (*although*) introduces the dependent clause.

Underline the dependent clause in each sentence. Circle each subordinating conjunction.

1. Because the leaves that they eat are only an arm's length away, sloths do not need to move quickly to feed themselves.

2. If you look at London's Big Ben clock tower, you will have an idea of how tall some giant redwood trees are.

3. So they could have a closer trim, Neanderthal males switched from tweezing their beards with seashells to shaving with flint blades.

4. While you may like baseball, soccer is the most watched sport in the world.

5. Although it may disgust you, worm composting produces nutrient-rich soil.

6. Because the giant yellowleg centipede of South America has potent venom, it can easily capture and eat a mouse.

7. Ali Bahcetepe of Turkey broke 698 concrete blocks with his fist in less than 30 seconds because he wanted to break the world record.

8. Because the world's largest cupcake was so large, it required 13 hours to bake.

9. Because a popcorn kernel's shell is waterproof, steam is trapped inside until it explodes.

10. Although their ears help radiate Africa's heat, elephants sometimes spray water from their trunks for a cool shower.

Name _____ Date _____

Review: Prepositions and Conjunctions

Circle each preposition.

1. Jupiter's moon, called Europa, may have an ocean under its ice-covered surface.

2. A female octopus lays eggs in long strands that she hangs from the roof of an underwater cave.

3. It is summer in the Northern Hemisphere when the northern half of Earth is tilted toward the sun.

4. At the back of the inner eye is light-sensitive tissue called the retina.

5. Thousands of years ago, the first people settling in North America may have come across the Bering land bridge.

Underline each conjunction. Then, write above each conjunction CL for correlative, CD for coordinating, or S for subordinating.

6. Although you see lightning first, thunder and lightning occur at the same time.

7. Ostriches do not need to drink fluids because they can both produce their own water and consume water from vegetation.

8. Vibration is a back-and-forth movement, and it produces light, heat, and sound.

9. Because the architecture of the Whispering Gallery allows sound to travel, a whisper can be heard 118 feet (36 m) away in Saint Paul's Cathedral in London.

10. Because sound generally travels faster through solids than gases, it travels about 14 times faster through iron than air.

Science Factoid: An echo is formed when sound waves reflect back to the listener. However, you cannot hear an echo in a small room because the walls are too close to the sound source. Because you can only hear an echo if sounds are more than one-fifteenth of a second apart, close walls do not produce an echo.

Name _____ Date _____

A prefix is a group of letters added to the beginning of a word.

- A **prefix** changes the meaning of a word.

Example: At the time it was built, the largest tracked land <u>transport</u> vehicle, called a crawler <u>transporter</u>, carried NASA rockets to the launchpad.

This is like breaking a code! First, you figure out that *trans-* means *across*. So, *transport* means *to carry something across* or *from one place to another.*

Circle the prefix in each underlined word. Use a dictionary to help you write the definition of each underlined word.

1. Submarines fill two sets of tanks with water to help them <u>descend</u> and replace the water with air to resurface. _____

   _____

2. Bronze artifacts have been protected from rust for more than 3,000 years because they have remained <u>submerged</u> in Slovenia's riverbanks. _____

   _____

3. The orderly pattern of atoms in a crystal <u>repeat</u> again and again. _____

   _____

4. It may sound <u>improbable</u>, but the neurons in your brain create and send more messages than all of the phones worldwide. _____

   _____

5. One type of <u>prehistoric</u> fish had a swordlike snout, knifelike teeth, and a pectoral fin like a saw._____

   _____

6. For more sun <u>protection</u>, use sunscreen with a higher SPF number. _____

   _____

7. It is a common <u>mistake</u> to mispronounce words ending in *-ough* because *-ough* can be said at least seven different ways. _____

   _____

Name _____ Date _____

A <u>suffix</u> is a group of letters added to the end of a word.

- A **suffix** changes the meaning of a word.

Example: Once again, you have mispronounced the word <u>zoo</u>logy.

The suffix is the tail end of a word. So, because -*ology* means *the study or science of* and *zoo-* means *animals*, what have you got? (By the way, the word is pronounced *zoh*-ology, not *zew*-ology. Impress your friends!)

Circle the suffix in each underlined word.

1. A diamond graded as FL is completely <u>flawless</u>.

2. <u>Librarians</u> use the Dewey decimal system to organize books in libraries.

3. Some <u>aquatic</u> birds can remain underwater for long periods without breathing.

4. Although she could not read, Abraham Lincoln's stepmother encouraged his love of books during his <u>childhood</u>.

5. In the Middle Ages, housewives brought their own dough to the <u>baker</u>, who would bake it in his oven.

6. In ancient Egypt, it was <u>fashionable</u> to wear woven papyrus sandals.

7. U.S. President Franklin Roosevelt's dog starred in a movie and was made an <u>honorary</u> private in the Army.

8. Both the leafy sea dragon and the weedy sea dragon use camouflage for <u>protection</u>.

9. In Mali, Africa, a griot is a <u>traveling</u> storyteller who shares the history of his people.

10. Hot <u>lemonade</u> has been used to fight flu-like illnesses since Roman times.

History Factoid: Alexander Graham Bell educated people who were deaf. He helped in the development of early recording devices. In 1874, Bell's phonautograph drew the vibrations of a human voice so that students could visualize sound. Two years later, Bell invented the telephone. His invention has revolutionized the way that people communicate.

Name _____ Date _____

A <u>sentence</u> is a group of words that express a complete thought.

• A complete sentence always has a **subject** and a **predicate**.

complete subject

Example: The first laundromat opened in the United States in 1934.

complete predicate

OK, let's talk to ourselves about this! *Who or what is the sentence about?* (That's the subject.) *What did it or they do?* (That's the predicate.) If it doesn't have both, it's not a complete sentence!

Write C beside each complete sentence. Write I beside each incomplete sentence.

1. _____ The large upper leg bone connecting the lower bones to the pelvis.

2. _____ One of the world's largest and loudest musical instruments is an organ in Atlantic City.

3. _____ The world's oil supply, perhaps.

4. _____ A crow, a cow, a hippopotamus, and a cat.

5. _____ If your body uses more water than you take in, you will become dehydrated.

6. _____ The Earth spins 360 degrees every 24 hours.

7. _____ Bubbles from carbon dioxide.

8. _____ Gases have no shape of their own.

9. _____ I do.

10. _____ A supernova is an exploding star.

Joke Break:
Hotel owner: "A room costs 50 dollars a night. It costs 30 dollars if you make your own bed."
Man: "Fine. I will make my own bed."
Hotel owner: "OK. I will get the wood and nails."

A <u>sentence</u> must have correct end punctuation.

- A **declarative sentence** ends with a period (.).
- An **interrogative sentence** ends with a question mark (?).
- An **exclamatory sentence** ends with an exclamation point (!).
- An **imperative sentence** may end with either a period or an exclamation point.

Examples: A swift is a type of bird that eats insects that it catches in the air.

Did you know that swifts use their saliva to glue their nests together?

Wow, that's amazing!

Look at that swift roosting on a brick wall.

I do declare that a statement must have a period.

Write a period, a question mark, or an exclamation point at the end of each sentence.

1. Adults laugh an average of 17 times a day

2. Scientists think that the first humans laughed as a sign of relief from passing danger

3. When we laugh, our brains direct us to make a set of gestures and produce a sound

4. Have you heard that laughing causes changes in your arms, legs, and trunk muscles

5. Fifteen facial muscles move whenever a person laughs

6. Laugh, and you'll notice the movement of your upper lip muscle

7. Wow, it is so strange that laughing can make you cry

8. Other than humans, which species of animals can laugh

9. Did you know that apes have their own form of laughter

10. Hey, don't monkey around with me

Science Factoid: Have you heard the one about the penguin in the wet suit? Don't laugh! This is not a joke! An African penguin in California suddenly began to shed his feathers. What could help the cold penguin that had lost his natural insulation? A diving gear supplier stepped in to make a miniature wet suit that fastened around the penguin's back.

A simple <u>simple subject</u> is the main noun or pronoun in a complete sentence.

- The **simple subject** names the main person, place, thing, or idea that the sentence is about.

Example: Possibly the first people to domesticate the cat, early <u>Egyptians</u> worshipped a cat goddess.

The simple subject is always a noun or pronoun. Ask yourself: *What is the one word that this whole sentence is about?* Answer: *Egyptians!* (Now, wasn't that simple?)

Circle the simple subject of each sentence.

1. Liquids have volume but no fixed shape.

2. The largest airplane in the world has a wingspan of nearly 320 feet (97.5 m).

3. The Great Barrier Reef caused many shipwrecks before it was mapped in the 1800s.

4. Before the invention of paper, people wrote on clay, bamboo, stone, and papyrus.

5. Hypocretin, a chemical in the brain, helps control how awake a person is.

6. The first car, built in 1769, had a steam engine.

7. The Department of Defense is America's oldest and largest government agency.

8. Some ancient civilizations used salt as money.

9. Black surfaces absorb more light than they reflect.

10. The largest flying reptile had a wingspan of nearly 40 feet (12.2 m).

Science Factoid: The quagga was a mammal related to the plains zebra. The quagga's body was striped only on the front part and was solid brown on its hindquarters. Once common in South Africa, this creature became extinct in 1883.

The simple predicate is the main verb contained in the complete predicate.

• The **simple predicate** expresses the main action or state of being of the subject.

Example: Lightning on Saturn <u>creates</u> powerful radio waves.

Ask yourself: *What's the action in this sentence? "Lightning on Saturn" does what? Answer: creates!*

Circle each simple predicate.

1. The average bald eagle can see a rabbit up to 3 miles (4.8 km) away.

2. A giant concave mirror in France produces temperatures of more than 7,200°F (4,000°C).

3. In 1610, Galileo saw Jupiter's moons through his telescope.

4. At night, the land cools faster than the sea.

5. Giraffes eat leaves from 20-foot (6-meter) high acacia trees.

6. The ice at the South Pole measures about 9,000 feet (2,700 m) deep.

7. Female lions work together as predators against large grassland animals.

8. Peregrine falcons dive at speeds of more than 200 miles (322 km) per hour.

9. Japanese scientists found an 87-million-year-old praying mantis fossil in a piece of amber.

10. More than 500,000 gallons (1,892,706 L) of water per second flow down Niagara Falls.

History Factoid: On December 1, 1955, police in Montgomery, Alabama, arrested Rosa Parks, an African American woman, because she refused to give her bus seat to a white man. This was against the law in many southern states. Parks' arrest sparked a bus boycott. For one year, almost 70 percent of Montgomery's bus riders used other transportation. Rosa Parks and the successful Montgomery bus boycott advanced the progress of racial equality in the United States.

Name _____ Date _____

A complete sentence may have one or more compound subjects or compound predicates.

- A **compound subject** contains two or more subjects that are joined by a conjunction and have the same verb.
- A **compound predicate** contains two or more verbs that are joined by a conjunction and have the same subject.

1 subject + 1 subject = compound subject.
1 verb + 1 verb = compound predicate. It's grammar math!
(Tip: Look for conjunctions!)

Example: Pierre and Marie Curie ←——— compound subject

discovered radium in 1902 and
received the Nobel Prize the next year. ←—— compound predicate

Circle each compound subject and underline each compound predicate.

1. Queen Cleopatra and Roman General Marc Antony married and maintained power over Egypt.

2. In 1778, an iron ladder was lost on an Alpine glacier and was found 44 years later in a different location.

3. Dian Fossey developed an interest in mountain gorillas and studied them for years.

4. Hurricanes, typhoons, and tropical cyclones are names given to the same phenomenon.

5. The Great Salt Lake exists in a dry environment and is saltier than the ocean.

6. Hemochromatosis turns the skin a bronze color and damages the body's organs.

7. Howard Hughes built and flew an airplane with the world's largest wingspan.

8. In the 1930s, Joseph Friedman invented and then mass-produced the bendable straw.

9. Spring peepers and American robins both announce the arrival of spring.

10. The female python laid her eggs and coiled her body around the eggs for warmth.

Science Factoid: What looks like an owl, stands like a penguin, and walks like a duck? The answer is a kakapo, the heaviest parrot in the world. These giant, flightless birds weigh about 9 pounds (4 kg) and grow to 25 inches (64 cm) tall.

A **direct object** is a noun or a pronoun that comes after an action verb.

- The **direct object** receives the action of the verb or shows the result of the action.

  verb   direct object

  Example: Broccoli contains selenium, which is a cancer-fighting element.

Broccoli contains what? Chocolate? No, it contains selenium! So, *selenium* is the direct object. See how the direct object always comes after the verb?

Circle each direct object.

1. About 40,000 spider species eat meat.

2. Spiders usually eat insects, larvae, fish, and even other spiders.

3. However, scientists recently discovered a species of vegetarian spiders.

4. These tropical jumping spiders eat mostly the buds on acacia plants.

5. Acacia plants grow sharp, hollow thorns.

6. These hollow thorns create a home for a species of ants.

7. The jumping spiders used the thorns as steps so that they could collect the plant buds.

8. Their skillful hunting style avoids the highly aggressive ants.

9. The spiders occasionally may eat ant larvae.

10. But, they prefer to eat the nutrient-rich acacia buds.

Joke Break:
Patient: "Doctor, Doctor, I swallowed my pen. What should I do?"
Doctor: "You should use a pencil!"

Name _____ Date _____

The indirect object always comes between the verb and the direct object of a sentence.

• The **indirect object** tells *to whom* or *for whom* the action of the verb is done.

More trickiness here! First, find the subject and verb. Then, ask: *What did he throw?* Answer: *The ball* (direct object). Then, ask: *To whom or for whom did he throw the ball?* Answer: *To the batter* (indirect object). Got it?

verb
↓

Example: The pitcher <u>threw</u> the
<u>batter</u> a wicked curve <u>ball</u>.
            ↑   ↑
      indirect object   direct object

Circle each indirect object.

1. The leopard fed her cubs antelope meat that was hidden in the tree.

2. A howler monkey's 30-inch (76-cm) tail gives it the strength to hang easily from trees.

3. The teacher told me that UVA rays weaken the immune system.

4. The ancient Greeks offered the Trojans a wooden horse.

5. In Wales, on Valentine's Day, people give their sweethearts carved wooden spoons.

6. The female honey badger fed her cubs a gerbil.

7. Eleven-year-old Grace Bedell wrote Abraham Lincoln a letter and asked him to grow a beard.

8. During courtship, the male hanging fly offers the female a large dead insect.

9. In the 1940s, men began giving women diamond engagement rings.

10. In the 1600s, a Mogul ruler built his wife the Taj Mahal as a memorial.

Joke Break:
Joe: "Will you make me a milkshake?"
Maggie: "Abracadabra, you're a milkshake!"

A <u>run-on sentence</u> occurs when two independent sentences are joined without proper punctuation.

- To correct a run-on sentence, make each independent sentence a separate sentence. Then, add end punctuation.

Example: Many fabrics are made from natural fibers for example clothes can be made from bamboo. (run-on sentence)

Many fabrics are made from natural fibers. For example, clothes can be made from bamboo. (two sentences)

Whew! That first line in the example had too much coffee! It has two complete thoughts that run together with no punctuation! You need to use a period or a conjunction to slo-o-o-w down and separate the two ideas.

Write *R* beside each run-on sentence.

1. _____ During one day, you will blink about 15,000 times.

2. _____ A ringhal cobra, native to Africa, spits venom.

3. _____ Early man used atlatls, sticks for launching spears, to hunt game.

4. _____ Using a computer, a man typed 67 books backward he set a world record.

5. _____ The world's most poisonous animal is a jellyfish its venom could kill 60 people.

6. _____ Bamboo is a sustainable resource it can be regrown quickly and reharvested.

7. _____ Blue ribbon eels are strange-looking fish with nostrils that look like fans.

8. _____ Boa constrictors have distinctive markings on their bodies, such as patterns of ovals, diamonds, circles, or jagged lines in a variety of colors.

History Factoid: In the early 1950s, paint-by-numbers became a popular pastime for young and old alike. A paint-by-number kit contained two brushes and up to 90 numbered jars of paints ready to be applied to a preprinted, numbered canvas. By 1954, the manufacturer had sold 12 million kits. Some people loved the idea that anyone could be an artist. Critics condemned the craft as a mindless activity that encouraged conformity.

Name _____ Date _____

A <u>sentence fragment</u> does not express a complete thought. It is not a complete sentence.

- A **complete sentence** must have a subject and a predicate and must express a complete thought.

Example: Can be up to several hundred miles thick. (sentence fragment)

Alpine glaciers can be up to several hundred miles thick. (complete sentence)

A fragment reads like someone fell asleep right in the middle of a thought. I hate it when . . . *zzzzz.*

Write *F* beside each sentence fragment. Write *C* beside each complete sentence.

1. _____   Armadillos are closely related to sloths and anteaters.

2. _____   In 1853, Chef George Crum may have accidentally invented the potato chip when trying to please a complaining customer.

3. _____   Volcanoes erupt.

4. _____   Hiking on glaciers, which often hide many crevasses.

5. _____   Decaffeinated coffee still contains some caffeine.

6. _____   Tree roots are strong enough to break rock.

7. _____   Many toys made of cast iron in the early 1900s.

8. _____   In 1969, engineers "turned off" Niagara Falls on the American side.

9. _____   Earth pillars, rocks standing on top of columns of dirt.

10. _____   Will create horizontal spinning within a storm cell.

Joke Break:
Question: What do you call cheese that is not yours?
Answer: "Nacho" cheese.

Name _____ Date _____

Review: Run-on Sentences and Sentence Fragments

Write *R* for run-on sentence, *F* for sentence fragment, or *C* for complete sentence.

1. _____ A geode is a hollow in a rock, it contains crystals.

2. _____ People eat leaves such as cabbage and lettuce.

3. _____ Because the dry climate has helped preserve the ruins of several ancient civilizations.

4. _____ Hot tubs can be a source of harmful bacteria.

5. _____ Made by the limestone skeletons of many tiny animals.

6. _____ Coral reefs require water temperatures above 64.4°F (18°C), also the water must be clear and unpolluted.

7. _____ A type of wasp paralyzes a tarantula with its sting and lays an egg inside the spider's body.

8. _____ Found buried in a network of caves in Austria.

9. _____ People need vocal cords to speak.

10. _____ Like a carrot, a mango contains.

11. _____ Although plants convert the sun's energy into chemical energy.

12. _____ Compass termites live in Australia they build large towers that always face north and south.

Joke Break:
Question: Why don't oysters donate to charities?
Answer: Because they're "shellfish."

Name _____ Date _____

It's is a <u>contraction</u>. Its is a <u>possessive pronoun</u>.

- *It's* is short for *it is*. *It's* is spelled with an apostrophe.
- *Its* shows ownership. *Its* is not spelled with an apostrophe.

Examples: A goldfish broke a world record for <u>its</u> ability to do tricks.

Because <u>it's</u> so smart, the owners named it Einstein.

In your head, substitute every *its* with *it is*. If *it is* makes sense, use an apostrophe. If *it is* doesn't make sense, keep your apostrophe to yourself!

Circle each correct word choice in parentheses.

1. (Its, It's) true that to survive winter, many insects produce glycerol, which acts like antifreeze.

2. The heaviest egg laid by a living bird is the ostrich egg; (its, it's) weight can exceed 5 pounds (2 kg).

3. Although a blackboard is generally green, (its, it's) name comes from (its, it's) original material, which was slate.

4. A beetle is appreciated by gardeners because of (its, it's) ability to eat dead leaves and other waste matter.

5. (Its, It's) likely that suntanning can cause premature wrinkles.

6. When (its, it's) threatened, the hawk moth caterpillar raises (its, it's) head and inflates (its, it's) thorax to look like the head of a snake.

7. Nomura's jellyfish of Japan grows to 6.5 feet (2 m), and (its, it's) weight can approach 450 pounds (204 kg).

8. An igloo built in Canada is so big that two cars could fit in (its, it's) interior.

Science Factoid: The crown-of-thorns starfish lives along coral reefs. It's one of the largest sea stars in the world. Its chief food source is coral polyps. It climbs onto coral reef structures where its stomach projects out of its mouth so that it can feast on the delicate polyps. Unfortunately, it's causing the destruction of coral reefs.

The subject and the verb must agree with each other in number.

- Usually, if the subject is singular, the verb ends in *-s*.
- Usually, if the subject is plural, the verb does not end in *-s*.

Examples: Earth rotates 180 degrees in 12 hours.

Strong winds, called jet streams, blow between the upper part of the troposphere and the stratosphere.

Air has weight.

Some verbs can play tricks on you. You have to learn these tricky guys by heart. For example, *is* becomes *are*, or *was* becomes *were* in the past tense.

Circle each correct verb in parentheses.

1. The sun's rays (is, are) weakest at the poles.

2. Green plants (use, uses) mainly the red and blue light bands of the spectrum.

3. Light (travel, travels) in straight lines.

4. My mother and father (says, say) that gravity keeps the atmosphere from floating away.

5. The atmosphere (is, are) made of four main layers—the troposphere, the stratosphere, the mesosphere, and the thermosphere.

6. How (do, does) scientists explain Earth's magnetic poles?

7. The inner core, a solid iron ball, (spin, spins) faster than the earth above it.

8. The outer core, which is molten, (churn, churns) like an ocean of iron.

9. It (act, acts) like a giant dynamo creating electricity.

10. Did you know that the stratosphere (contain, contains) the ozone layer?

Science Factoid: The ichneumon "fly" is actually a wasp. When it is ready to reproduce, the wasp captures a caterpillar. Then, it injects its eggs into the body of the caterpillar. Upon hatching, the wasp's larvae eat the host from the inside out.

Name _____ Date _____

- The **main verb** must agree with the **main subject** of the sentence.

Example: After the asteroid hit, the

herd of dinosaurs was unable

to survive.

Wait a minute! *Dinosaurs* is not the subject here! That's pretty tricky, huh? The subject is *herd*. *Of dinosaurs* is a prepositional phrase, but I bet you already knew that!

Underline each subject. Then, circle each correct verb in parentheses.

1. The vibrations of an earthquake (are, is) called seismic waves.

2. Those insects high in the tree (see, sees) ultraviolet light, but we cannot.

3. In 1814, an army of British soldiers (was, were) able to seize the U.S. capital of Washington, D.C.

4. Often, a flock of passenger pigeons (contain, contains) hundreds of thousands of birds.

5. A double-decker bus, which has two floors, (is, are) commonly used in England.

6. The sound waves in this classroom (create, creates) a moving pattern of molecules in the air.

7. A group of owls (is, are) called a parliament.

8. Even though they are not edible, the leaves of the poinsettia plant (is, are) not poisonous.

9. Classroom chalk, once made from tiny shells, (is, are) now made from a mineral called gypsum.

10. Sudden changes in weather usually (occur, occurs) along the boundaries between air masses.

Science Factoid: Objects dropped at the North Pole or the South Pole fall faster than objects dropped at the equator. Because Earth spins on its axis, it bulges slightly at the equator. These rotations cause Earth to be flatter at the poles. So, an object at one of the poles is closer to Earth's center of gravity. Therefore, an object experiences a stronger gravitational pull at the poles than an object at the equator.

The subject and the verb must agree with each other in number.

- A **compound subject** contains two or more subjects that have the same verb. The subjects are joined by a conjunction.
- A compound subject connected by the words *or* or *nor* requires a singular verb.

Example: According to some scientists, either volcanic activity or an asteroid was responsible for wiping out the dinosaurs.

Only one event wiped out the dinosaurs, not both of them. Notice the word *either*? That means that the subject is singular and needs the singular verb *was*.

Underline each subject. Then, circle each correct verb in parentheses.

1. When your leg falls asleep, a burning feeling or tingling (tells, tell) you to move your leg before you suffer nerve damage.

2. Some people think either a parrot or a mynah (is, are) the easiest bird to train to talk.

3. Dry weather and drought (contribute, contributes) to dangerous wildfires.

4. Neither the raven nor the blue jay (eat, eats) a strictly vegetarian diet.

5. Luke and Amanda (is, are) standing about 4,000 miles (6,437 km) from Earth's center.

6. Neither Mahatma Gandhi nor Dr. Martin Luther King Jr. (was, were) in support of violence.

7. Either an amethyst or an opal (is, are) part of the British Crown Jewels.

8. My mother and father (tell, tells) me that a person's height decreases by the end of the day.

9. Viruses and bacteria (is, are) prevented from entering your body through the skin, an important part of your immune system.

10. Both a python and a boa (has, have) an extra organ on their heads that detect heat sources in their surroundings.

A <u>subject</u> and a <u>verb</u> agree if both are singular or both are plural.

- **Indefinite pronouns**, such as *someone*, *somebody, anyone, everyone,* and *each*, are singular.
- Indefinite pronouns, such as *several, few, both,* and *many,* are plural.

Example: The Galápagos Islands are home to the largest living tortoises, and <u>each</u> <u>is</u> protected by law.

You're really saying that each individual tortoise is protected, so you need the singular verb, *is*.

Underline each subject pronoun. Then, circle each correct verb in parentheses.

1. Until 2005, no one (was, were) aware of a species of flesh-eating caterpillars.

2. Of all moths and butterflies, a few (is, are) predators, and all of those (eat, eats) other insects.

3. Many still (think, thinks) it is strange that one species of caterpillar will eat only snails.

4. If anyone (wonder, wonders) where these caterpillars live, they inhabit the Hawaiian Islands.

5. Several tests have been performed, and each (show, shows) that flesh-eating caterpillars refuse to eat lichens, carrots, and all other caterpillar foods.

6. The caterpillars wait for snails to rest on leaves and then poke each snail to make sure that it (is, are) alive.

7. Using silk webbing, the caterpillars quickly bind their prey to the leaves until each snail (is, are) tied down.

8. Reaching into the live snail's shell, the caterpillar begins eating its flesh until none (is, are) left.

9. Some caterpillars then (attach, attaches) the empty snail shells onto their casings as a form of camouflage.

10. Scientists do not know why these caterpillars exist nowhere else on the planet, but some (think, thinks) it is because Hawaii is so isolated from the rest of the world.

Name _____ Date _____

A <u>subject</u> and a <u>verb</u> agree
if both are singular or both are plural.

- A singular noun follows the clause *there is*.
- A plural noun follows the clause *there are*.

Examples: <u>There is</u> that <u>plant</u> which is known to
eat birds, small lizards, and rodents.

<u>There are</u> those strange <u>mounds</u>
of earth, or pingos, that are seen in
permafrost areas.

Look at number 7.
When you have a
compound subject
(1 subject + 1 subject),
use the plural verb *are*.

Circle each correct clause in parentheses.

1. (There is, There are) the raccoon that has been opening our trash can.

2. (There is, There are) the map of killer bees in the southern United States.

3. (There is, There are) the instructions for putting together your bike.

4. (There is, There are) the fly that has been buzzing around the room all day.

5. (There is, There are) the 13 items that I have chosen for my baker's dozen.

6. (There is, There are) the tigers that live in the jungles of Asia.

7. (There is, There are) the high tide and low tide marks that appear about every 12 hours.

8. (There is, There are) the white-tailed doe and her two fawns grazing in the meadow.

9. (There was, There were) the old photo of a dodo from the island of Mauritius.

10. (There was, There were) the hoofprints of the deer that had been feasting in my garden.

Science Factoid: The guest speaker narrated her video by saying, "There is a male bowerbird. He attracts his mate by decorating his nest. Male bowerbirds of New Guinea and Australia create large, elaborate nests decorated with flowers and colorful objects. There are other birds that paint their nests with a mixture of saliva and berry juice."

Name _____ Date _____

A <u>pronoun</u> and the noun that it replaces must agree with each other.

- A pronoun and the noun that it replaces must agree in number and gender.

                              subject
                                 ↓
Examples: <u>Marsupial frogs</u> have a pouch,

            and <u>they</u> store eggs in this pouch.

pronoun————————↑

            <u>One</u> should wipe <u>his</u> shoes before

            entering the house.

Gender means male or female, so use *he* for males and *she* for females. If you use *one*, then match it with either *he* or *she*, like the second example. (*Gremlins* never wear shoes, so I know they're not talking to *us!*)

Underline each subject. Circle each correct pronoun and each correct verb in parentheses.

1. The Andean condor has the largest wingspan of any bird of prey, and (she, they) (produce, produces) one chick every two years.

2. Mouthbreeders are fish, and (they, it) (shelter, shelters) their babies in their mouths.

3. Siamese fighting fish live in the lakes of Southeast Asia, and (it, they) (make, makes) their nests from bubbles.

4. Both a compass and a GPS are navigational tools, but (it, they) (has, have) different capabilities.

5. Metal is a good conductor of heat, which explains why (it, they) (feel, feels) cold to the touch.

6. One must learn to identify animal prints if (they, he) (is, are) planning to track animals in the wild.

7. Everyone should turn off unnecessary lights if (she, they) (want, wants) to conserve energy.

8. Elephants can be either Asian or African, but (it, they) (is, are) always herbivores.

Name _____ Date _____

Review: Subject and Verb Agreement

Circle each correct word choice in parentheses.

1. The Amazon River, which is in South America, (carry, carries) 20 percent of the world's freshwater.

2. Either osmium or iridium (is, are) the heaviest metal in the world.

3. A bowling ball on the moon (weigh, weighs) less than on Earth.

4. The skin on our bodies (is, are) our largest organ.

5. There (is, are) a group of oyster larvae, also called a spat.

6. Scott and Doug correctly (believe, believes) that the saber-toothed cat lived 10,000 years ago.

7. The first horse, a creature called eohippus, (was, were) only about 10 inches (25 cm) high.

8. If someone has a condition called hairy tongue, (they, she) can cure it with antibiotics.

9. On average, an American family (wash, washes) about 300 loads of laundry per year.

10. Has anyone seen a porpoise, and can (he, they) tell me how they differ from dolphins, besides having a rounder snout?

11. Every clam has a shell, and (it, they) may be hard or soft.

12. Frogs differ from toads because (she, they) have moist, shiny skin.

History Factoid: French brothers Auguste and Louis Lumiere are known for making the first film shown to an audience. The movie was played in Paris in 1895. Everyone in the crowd was amazed. One scene featuring an oncoming train was so realistic that many audience members ran from the theater in fear.

Name _____ Date _____

The describing word _good_ is always an adjective.
The describing word __well__ can be an adjective or an adverb.

- The word _good_ can be part of the subject or part of the predicate. It may be used with a linking verb, such as, _look, feel (touch), sound, taste,_ or _be,_ to describe the subject.
- The describing word _well_ can be an adverb or an adjective.
- The adverb _well_ describes someone's or something's actions.

Just remember that you always do something _well._ You never do something _good._ How _well_ did you understand that?

Examples: Some people think that Charlie Chaplin was a <u>good</u> actor.

Some people think that Charlie Chaplin acted <u>well</u>.

In each sentence, circle the correct describing word in parentheses.

1. How do ballet dancers spin so (good, well), especially on traditional pointe shoes, without becoming dizzy?

2. Forecasting tornadoes (good, well) is more difficult than predicting hurricanes.

3. The Arabian horse, a breed developed in the desert, has (good, well) endurance.

4. After misusing his golden touch in the famous myth, King Midas learned his lesson (good, well).

5. Although Wagner's opera, _The Ring_, may be a (good, well) opera to hear, it lasts for four days!

6. Janet Guthrie drove so (good, well) that she was the first woman to drive in the Indy 500.

History Factoid: Joseph Turner, a British painter, wanted to paint a realistic picture of a storm at sea. One day, in the early 1800s, he asked sailors to tie him well to the mast of a ship during a storm. In this way, he thought he would have a good view of the storm and would be able to appreciate its fury.

Name _____ Date _____

The describing word _bad_ is always an adjective.
The describing word _badly_ is always an adverb.

- The word _bad_ can be part of the subject or part of the predicate. It may be used with a linking verb, such as _look, feel (touch), sound, taste,_ or _be,_ to describe the subject.
- The word _badly_ describes someone's or something's actions.

This one can be tricky! A person always does something _badly,_ not _bad._ Also, a person feels _bad,_ not _badly._ Learn this and sound smart!

Examples: A man was <u>badly</u> injured when a tarantula shot a cloud of tiny hairs into his eyes.

I had a <u>bad</u> dream after I read about ancient Egyptian crocodile mummies.

In each sentence, circle the correct describing word in parentheses.

1. The story of the Cherry Sisters shows how these (bad, badly) entertainers became a successful vaudeville act.

2. Vaudeville, a type of talent show in the late 1800s, contained comedy acts, theater, and music of both good and (bad, badly) quality.

3. Large audiences attended the shows, and when they did not like an act, they sometimes behaved (bad, badly).

4. Some people threw rotten vegetables and eggs at vaudeville acts that performed (bad, badly) on stage.

5. The five Cherry Sisters knew that they were (bad, badly) singers, actors, and songwriters.

6. But, they (bad, badly) needed money to save their Iowa farm after their parents died.

7. In their 1890s vaudeville act, the Cherry Sisters sang so (bad, badly) that they had to place a net between themselves and the audience.

8. The famous producer Oscar Hammerstein heard about their (bad, badly) performances and brought them to Broadway.

9. Crowds packed the theater every night, but the Cherry Sisters became most famous when they sued a newspaper for printing a (bad, badly) review of their act.

Name _____ Date _____

Avoid using a double negative in a sentence.

- A **double negative** is the use of two negative words in a sentence when one is sufficient.
- Examples of negative words include *not, no, never, nothing, nobody,* and *none.*

Example: Identical twins <u>can't never</u> be the opposite sex. (incorrect)

Identical twins <u>can never</u> be the opposite sex. (correct)

The words *never* and *can't* are negative words. Never use two negative words together.

Underline the negative words in each sentence. Then, write C beside each sentence that uses a negative correctly.

1. _____ In the animal world, multiple births are not never called twins, triplets, or quadruplets.

2. _____ It does not matter which species of animal babies is being discussed, because multiples are always referred to as a litter.

3. _____ In human births, identical twins are not more common than fraternal twins.

4. _____ Fraternal twins aren't no more similar than regular brothers and sisters.

5. _____ I have never seen no identical twins that were impossible to tell apart.

6. _____ Even identical twins aren't never exactly the same because people have different personalities.

7. _____ No one can't know for sure, but heredity, nutrition, and the mother's age may contribute to having fraternal twins.

8. _____ Studies show identical twins don't never read each other's minds even though they may sometimes think alike.

Science Factoid: Two-headed snakes are sometimes born but seldom survive in the wild. One such bull snake was donated to the St. Louis Zoo and lived for more than two years. Zookeepers needed to place an index card between the snake's heads so that it would not fight with itself when eating!

Name _____ Date _____

Some verbs are easily confused with other verbs.

- The verb *sit* means *to rest* or *be seated*.
  The verb *set* means *to place something down*.
- The verb *lay* means *to put something down somewhere*.
  The verb *lie* means *to rest* or *to stretch out*.

Even grown-ups get confused on *lie* and *lay*. So, use this chart when you aren't sure if you're laying or lying!

	Present	Past	With Helping Verb
When I recline:	I *lie* down	I *lay* down	I *have lain* down
When I put something down:	I *lay* bricks	I *laid* bricks	I *have laid* bricks

Circle each correct verb in parentheses.

1. Japan, consisting of four large islands and more than 3,000 smaller ones, (lies, lays) off the east coast of Asia.

2. Japan's islands are the exposed tops of mountain chains that (lie, lay) deep on the ocean floor.

3. About 1542, Portuguese merchants (set, sat) sail and became Japan's first contact with Europeans.

4. In the 1600s, the Japanese expelled the Spanish and Portuguese and (sit, set) strict rules to maintain power.

5. In 1854, a U.S. Navy expedition under Commodore Matthew Perry (laid, lay) ships off the coast of Japan.

6. Commodore Perry and the Japanese agreed to (set, sit) up negotiations and were successful in opening two Japanese ports to trade with the United States.

7. To celebrate the arrival of Commodore Perry, many Japanese people today (sit, set) and watch fireworks on Black Ship Day.

Name _____ Date _____

Some verbs are easily confused with other verbs.

- The word *affect* is a verb. It means *to influence* or *change something*.
- The word *effect* is usually a noun. It means *the result of some action*.

Examples: Sunlight's heat, Earth's rotation, and land and water all <u>affect</u> the winds.

One <u>effect</u> of Earth's rotation is changing patterns of airflow.

The *effect* or the *affect*? Which is the noun? Here's a cool trick to help you remember: *The* ends with an *e*, and *effect* starts with an *e*, so that's the noun!

Circle each correct word choice in parentheses.

1. The (affect, effect) of making water cold is that the colder water sinks.

2. Nutrition (affects, effects) a person's health.

3. The calcium atoms of your bones absorb X-ray photons and keep them from penetrating, which (affects, effects) the X-ray image.

4. Some laundry soaps contain a special chemical to create a brighter (affect, effect).

5. The (affect, effect) of the oscilloscope is to turn light, radio, and sound waves into electrical patterns.

6. The gravity of massive objects can (affect, effect) light rays, causing them to bend.

7. Acromegaly is a disease that (affects, effects) the growth of a person's hands, feet, and face.

8. In Japan, the (affect, effect) of careful planting, cultivation, and harvesting methods is high crop yields.

9. Great excitement can (affect, effect) the size of a person's pupils.

History Factoid: In 46 BC, Emperor Julius Caesar created the Julian calendar. Then, in 1582, Pope Gregory XIII updated the Julian calendar by eliminating 10 days. That year, October 4 was followed by October 15. This change had the effect of allowing the new Gregorian calendar to align with the seasons. This is the calendar we still use today.

Some verbs are easily confused with other verbs.

- The verb *raise* means *to cause something to go up*.
  The verb *rise* means *to get up* or *to go up*.
- The verb *accept* means *to receive*.
  The preposition *except* means *to leave out* or *to exclude*.

Rise does not take a direct object. In other words, you can't rise something. But, you can raise something, like your hand!

Examples: Six soldiers raised the flag at Iwo Jima.

The phoenix, a mythical bird, would rise from the ashes.

U.S. President Barack Obama was asked to accept the Nobel Peace Prize in 2009.

Except for sponges, all animal cells are arranged into tissues.

Circle each correct word choice in parentheses.

1. Most planets in the solar system have at least one moon, (accept, except) Mercury and Venus.

2. At a lantern festival in Taiwan, people (raise, rise) lanterns to hope for good fortune in the new year.

3. Scientists are studying the (rise, raise) and fall of the Mayan Empire to help Guatemalan farmers.

4. Often, a horse will not (raise, rise) in the morning because it may sleep standing up.

5. Benjamin Franklin said, "Early to bed and early to (raise, rise) makes a man healthy, wealthy, and wise."

6. Do you (accept, except) the theory that time is related to the expansion of space?

7. To help with recycling, some manufacturers (accept, except) cans of leftover household paint to be reused.

8. States and countries (raise, rise) their flags to half-mast to honor those who gave their lives for their country.

Name _____ Date _____

Homophones have different meanings.

- A **homophone** is pronounced the same as another word, but it has a different meaning and spelling.

Example: An average person takes 20,000 breaths of <u>air</u> a day.

In some countries, when a king dies, the oldest male <u>heir</u> receives the crown.

Can you think of two homophones for *their*? *They're* right *there!*

Circle each correct word choice in parentheses.

1. The red color of a (beat, beet) comes from the betalain pigments, which can stain your hands and clothes.

2. A (bite, byte) is the basic unit of measurement for computer information storage.

3. If your vocal cords become irritated, your voice will sound (horse, hoarse).

4. A mule deer's antlers are covered with velvet that nourishes the bone until the antlers are fully (groan, grown).

5. Without a chain guard, a bike rider's pant leg may get stuck between the (pedal, peddle) and the chain.

6. The tiny (deer, dear) tick, or black-legged tick, spreads Lyme disease.

7. A San Diego college once offered a (coarse, course) called Underwater Basket Weaving.

8. A winter (night, knight) is a good time to study stars because the haze from summer's humidity is gone.

9. Jupiter completes one orbit around the sun every 4,333 (days, daze).

10. Female common cat (fleas, flees) lay up to 20 eggs per day on their host.

Fun Factoid: Geocaching is a game about searching for hidden treasure. By following the coordinates on a GPS receiver, the searchers find a container, or cache. The cache usually contains small items. Although the treasure is not cash, the thrill of the search makes geocaching a great adventure.

Name _____ Date _____

Some words are easily confused with other words.

- Some words have similar spellings or pronunciations.

Example: In the <u>past</u>, the number of bald eagles was shrinking, but Congress <u>passed</u> laws to protect them.

In this example, *past* refers to a previous time in history and *passed* is a verb. It's not exactly a homophone, because the endings sound a little different. But, it's still pretty tricky!

Circle each correct word choice in parentheses. Use a dictionary if you need help.

1. Some electric cars are (quite, quiet) (quiet, quite) so that pedestrians cannot hear them.

2. Oil collects in the (pours, pores) of human skin.

3. The planet (shown, shone) because it reflected the sun's light.

4. New fossils suggest that some dinosaurs had more interesting feathers (than, then) modern birds.

5. I (all ready, already) knew that fingernails grow faster in warm weather than in cold weather.

6. (Where, Wear) did you learn that drinking from reusable containers and recycling plastic water bottles help reduce waste and pollution?

7. A person can (lose, loose) 100 strands of hair every day.

8. The colors that are opposite each other on the color wheel, like red and green, are (complimentary, complementary).

9. Do you know (weather, whether) a freshwater leech has a mouth at each end of its body to attach to prey?

History Factoid: Sometimes myths and legends have more than a kernel of truth. Colonel Davy Crockett was a famous frontiersman from Tennessee. By his own account, he killed 105 bears in one year! More than 100 years after his death, his trademark coonskin cap with striped tail became a fad. The legend of Davy Crockett is a real-life tall tale.

Name _____ Date _____

A clause is a group of words that has a subject and a predicate and is used as part of a sentence.

- An **independent clause** is a complete sentence. It does not need other clauses to complete its thought.
- A **dependent clause** cannot stand alone as a sentence. A dependent clause needs an independent clause to complete its thought.

Look at number 2. It's a tricky one! The independent clause is split into two parts.

dependent clause ⟶

Example: To help strengthen teeth, fluoride is sometimes added to water. ⟵ independent clause

Underline each independent clause. Circle each dependent clause.

1. Human saliva contains the enzyme amylase, which helps digest food.

2. A jackrabbit, which is actually a hare, can leap about 45 miles (72 km) per hour.

3. A full-grown adult jackrabbit has 32 teeth, including four wisdom teeth.

4. Many bacteria have tails, which are called flagella.

5. Some cockroaches hiss when they fight.

6. Organisms need water because it helps them live and grow.

7. A golf ball can travel faster at high altitudes where there is less air resistance.

8. During heavy mountain snows, mail delivered in the early 1800s from Missouri to California could take 12 to 16 days.

9. To lure predators away from their nests, both the adult curlew and the plover pretend to be injured.

10. Although it may look like medication, a placebo is really a sugar pill.

Science Factoid: Because it measures about one-millionth of an inch (17 to 300 nanometers) across, a virus is about a thousand times smaller than bacteria. When a virus enters a human cell, it begins making new viruses. The cell will then burst, and the new viruses are released into the body to continue the process.

Name _____ Date _____

Details make a sentence more interesting.

- Use a **dependent clause** that begins with *who* or *whom* to describe people.
- Use a dependent clause that begins with *that* or *which* to describe things or animals.

Examples: Mathew Webb, <u>who</u> was a British sea captain, was the first person to swim across the English Channel.

Seaweed, <u>which</u> is a type of algae, does not have roots.

Confused about when to use *which* and when to use *that*? *Which* usually goes after a comma for less important information. *That* introduces more important stuff. It's a rule *that* you need to know, see?

Circle each correct word choice in parentheses.

1. The *Vickers Vimy*, (which, that) was flown by two British pilots, was the first plane to fly across the Atlantic.

2. Some scientists want to add savory and fat to the four basic tastes, (which, that) are sweet, salty, sour, and bitter.

3. Babe Ruth was a standout left-handed pitcher (who, that) could also hit.

4. In 1497, Vasco da Gama, (who, which) was Portuguese, was the first person to sail around Africa to India.

5. The stinging nettle (that, which) you touched released formic acid.

6. The cuttlefish, (which, that) uses camouflage to hide from danger, can fine-tune its color changes like a high-definition TV.

7. The Chunnel, (which, that) cost $15 billion to build, is an underwater tunnel connecting England to France.

8. Moss, (which, that) has little capsules full of spores, does not have flowers.

History Factoid: Francisco de Orellana, who was a Spanish explorer, gave the Amazon River its name. While exploring, Orellana reported seeing a group of female warriors, who reminded him of an ancient Greek myth. He called the river *Amazon*, the name that was given to the warriors in the myth.

Details make a sentence more interesting.

- A sentence often is more interesting when it tells *who* or *whom, what, when, where, why,* or *how.*

Example: Guinea worm disease is a tricky parasitic infestation.

Guinea worm disease is a tricky parasitic infestation <u>because its symptoms make diagnosis difficult.</u>

Because its symptoms make diagnosis difficult answers the question, *"Why?"* It gives important details and makes the sentence more interesting.

Write a new, more interesting sentence by answering each question in parentheses.

1. The baseball player threw the ball. (To whom?) _____

    _____

    _____

    _____

2. Steven climbed the tree. (Why?) _____

    _____

    _____

    _____

3. My friends and I met at one o'clock. (Why? Where?) _____

    _____

    _____

    _____

4. The bees swarmed. (How many? Why?) _____

    _____

    _____

    _____

5. The eagle opened its sharp claws. (Why?) _____

    _____

    _____

    _____

Name _____ Date _____

Details make a sentence more interesting.

- Use an **adjective clause** to describe a noun or a pronoun.
- Use an **adverb clause** to describe a verb, an adjective, or an adverb.

adjective clause

Examples: The insect <u>that bit the man</u> was a mosquito.

Water becomes a gas <u>when it reaches the boiling point of 212°F (100°C)</u>.

adverb clause

Get out your ice pack, because I've got a hot tip for you! Most adjective clauses begin with words like *that*, *who*, *whose*, or *which*. Most adverb clauses begin with words like *when*, *after*, *although*, or *since*.

Rewrite each sentence to make it more interesting. Use the hints in parentheses to add details.

1. The cat followed the man. (Which one? Add an adjective clause.) _____

_____

_____

2. The two dogs ran. (Why? Add an adverb clause.) _____

_____

_____

3. My brother dug up a worm. (Where? Add an adverb clause.) _____

_____

_____

4. The leaves fell from the tree. (Which one? Add an adjective clause.)_____

_____

_____

5. My dad replaced the roof. (Why? Add an adverb clause.) _____

_____

_____

6. She picked the berries. (Why? Add an adverb clause.)_____

_____

_____

Name _____ Date _____

A compound sentence consists of two or more independent clauses that are joined together.

- Join two sentences by using a conjunction, such as *and, but, or,* or *so.*
- Join two sentences by using a semicolon after the first sentence and a period after the second sentence.

Examples: Mount Kilimanjaro is in Africa, <u>and</u> it is the highest mountain on the continent.

Aye-ayes are rare primates that are nocturnal; they spend all day curled up in a ball-like nest.

A semicolon? Yes, semicolons are not scary and can be used by people ages 10 and up! Just *don't* use one with a conjunction; make sure you are connecting two complete sentences on the same topic.

Rewrite the underlined part of each sentence pair using a conjunction or a semicolon.

1. The Olympic Games have many different <u>events. Some</u> Olympic sports are unusual.

   _____

   _____

2. The ancient Olympic Games were supposed to build <u>diplomacy. The</u> games honored Zeus. _____

   _____

3. Beach volleyball was not a sport in the ancient Olympic <u>Games.</u> It was added at the 1996 Atlanta games. _____

   _____

4. Pole-vaulting started when men used poles to cross <u>canals. Distance</u> was more important than height. _____

   _____

5. The first Olympic torch relay was part of the summer games in <u>1936. It</u> was added to the winter games in 1952. _____

   _____

History Factoid: The first contact lenses were created in 1887 in Germany; they were big and heavy. They could be worn for only a few hours a day. In the 1950s, lenses were made of plastic, and they became smaller and thinner.

A run-on sentence occurs when two independent clauses are joined without proper punctuation.

- A run-on sentence may be corrected by making each independent clause a separate sentence and adding end punctuation.

Take the caffeine out of run-on sentences! Separate them into two sentences, and be sure to capitalize the first word in the second sentence.

Example: Earth once had one supercontinent a scientist named it Pangaea. (run-on)

Earth once had one supercontinent. A scientist named it Pangaea. (correct)

Rewrite each run-on sentence as two sentences.

1. The sunflower tracks the sun's movement this phenomenon is called heliotropism.

   _____

   _____

2. Argentina grows sunflowers the sunflower seed is Argentina's most important product.

   _____

   _____

3. Russia grows the most sunflowers the sunflower is its national flower.

   _____

   _____

4. Sunflowers are very fast growing in fact, they can grow up to 15 feet (4.5 m) tall.

   _____

   _____

5. Some experts believed that sunflowers first grew in what is now the eastern United States they were grown 4,000 to 5,000 years ago.

   _____

   _____

Food Factoid: In China, the hundred-year egg is a delicacy. To make these preserved eggs, a person first places an egg in a mixture of clay, ash, salt, and lime. Once the egg has lain there for several months, the yolk becomes dark green. The white becomes dark brown. The egg is then ready to be eaten.

A run-on sentence occurs when two independent clauses are joined without proper punctuation.

- A run-on sentence may be corrected by joining the two independent clauses with a conjunction, such as *and*, *but*, or *so*, or with a semicolon (;).

Do not fear the semicolon! When you separate two sentences with a semicolon, just remember that the second sentence doesn't need a capital letter.

Example: Earth contains seven continents and thousands of islands they total more than 50 million square miles (80 million sq. km) of land. (incorrect)

Earth contains seven continents and thousands of islands; they total more than 50 million square miles (80 million sq. km) of land. (correct)

Rewrite each run-on sentence using a conjunction or a semicolon.

1. Today, sunflowers are a practical crop with many uses sunflowers are among the top U.S. cash crops. _____

    _____

2. Sunflower products include cooking oil sunflower seeds are high in protein. _____

    _____

3. Sunflower roots can grow deep into polluted water systems they are able to take out large amounts of uranium and other toxic metals. _____

    _____

4. Sunflowers should be planted in sunny areas they need well-drained soil. _____

    _____

5. Sunflowers are salt resistant they grow on coastal beaches and dunes. _____

    _____

Science Factoid: Why are there so many craters on the moon compared to Earth? When the moon was formed, gases and water vapor were lost; this left the moon dry and airless. With no atmosphere, the moon has no weather and no erosion, so craters are not altered over time. Meteors have battered the moon for 4.4 billion years.

Name _____   Date _____

A sentence fragment is an incomplete thought. It is one part of a sentence punctuated as though it were a whole sentence.

- A **complete sentence** has a subject and a predicate and expresses a complete thought. ┌── subject

Example: The middle and fourth
fingernails grow faster than
the other fingernails.
└── predicate

When you read my joke at the bottom of the page, you'll notice that *Not very much!* is a sentence fragment. Sometimes a sentence fragment is used for a reason, like for a laugh!

Write complete sentences using the sentence fragments below and the suggestions in parentheses.

1. The snake in the grass. (Add a verb and a direct object.) _____

   _____

2. Creates a sculpture. (Add a subject.) _____

   _____

3. Sees the mouse. (Add a subject.) _____

   _____

4. James and Davis, who are friends, saw. (Add a direct object.) _____

   _____

5. Chases the kite. (Add a subject.) _____

   _____

6. Jumps over the ditch. (Add a subject.) _____

   _____

7. For twenty minutes and thirty seconds. (Add a subject and a predicate.)

   _____

   _____

Joke Break:
Teacher: "Ava, you missed school yesterday, didn't you?"
Ava: "Not very much!"

Name _____ Date _____

Review: Run-on Sentences and Sentence Fragments

Correct each run-on sentence or sentence fragment by writing a new sentence or sentences.

1. Paper money is inexpensive to make it costs only pennies to make one American dollar.

   _____

   _____

2. Buy shoes in the afternoon this is when a person's feet have expanded in size.

   _____

   _____

3. Sinus cavities are hollow they lie behind the forehead, eyes, and cheeks.

   _____

   _____

4. More than one billion Valentine's Day cards.

   _____

   _____

5. Viruses in the body are hard to kill laser light is a new approach.

   _____

   _____

6. Disposable diapers, which are creating environmental problems.

   _____

   _____

7. Because of strong winds.

   _____

   _____

Science Factoid: You may think that the bones in your body are white. Not always. The color of human and animal bones is usually beige or light brown. Museum workers clean and bleach the bones for display.

A <u>misplaced modifier</u> is a word, or a group of words, that is placed too far from the word or words that it describes.

- To avoid confusion, a describing word or phrase should be as near as possible to the word it describes.

Examples: Koalas eat <u>only</u> eucalyptus leaves.

Only Koalas eat eucalyptus leaves.

Misplaced modifiers make people confused or make them laugh. Is eucalyptus all that koalas eat? Or, are they the only animals that eat eucalyptus? See the difference? The meaning of the sentence changes depending on where you place the modifier!

Each misplaced modifier is underlined. Draw an arrow to show where each misplaced modifier should be placed.

1. <u>Only</u> cordless tools have been sold since the 1960s.

2. Because symptoms may be minor, <u>only</u> parents may notice a child's color blindness when he is learning colors.

3. Penicillin was discovered by Alexander Fleming in 1928 <u>accidentally</u>.

4. On a sunny day, <u>only</u> people can start a fire using a magnifying lens and tinder.

5. A male platypus has sharp spurs that secrete venom <u>on its rear feet</u>.

6. One person in every 1,000 can see <u>only</u> the indigo part of the light spectrum.

7. An ancient Roman artifact is in the museum <u>that is more than 2,000 years old</u>.

8. Nocturnal vampire bats prey on cows and horses that are often asleep <u>in South America</u>.

9. The Hope Diamond is on display at the Smithsonian Institution, <u>which was once owned by King Louis XIV of France</u>.

10. The golden wedding anniversary is celebrated after <u>only</u> 50 years of marriage.

Joke Break:
Little Sister: "Who just ran out of the house?"
Big Sister: "Daddy is running after the puppy in his bathrobe."
Little Sister: "Wow, I didn't know the puppy had a bathrobe!"

Name _____ Date _____

A dangling modifier is a phrase or clause that has no word to modify or describe.

- A **modifier** must be clearly related to some part of a sentence.

Examples: After adding the acetone, the foam cup melted into goop.

After adding the acetone, the scientist melted the foam cup into goop.

The first example is confusing! Did the foam cup add acetone to itself? I don't think so!

Rewrite each sentence so that the modifier clearly relates to the word or words in parentheses.

1. After traveling with soldiers into battle, many medals were received. (Stubby the dog)

   _____

   _____

2. Stroking with their wings as if flying underwater, small fish are hunted. (puffins)

   _____

   _____

3. While waiting for a donor heart, the Jarvik-7 artificial heart was received. (the patient)

   _____

   _____

4. Before a supernova occurs, the core is compressed. (the star's gravity)

   _____

   _____

5. Crawling above the ground at night, soil is consumed. (earthworms)

   _____

   _____

Joke Break:

Teacher: "Charlie, please tell us one interesting fact about James Madison, the fourth president of the United States."

Charlie: "At the age of one month, James Madison's nurse became concerned about his health."

Teacher: "A one-month-old nurse? Now, that is an interesting fact!"

Name _____ Date _____

Sentences can be written in the <u>first person</u>, the <u>second person</u>, or the <u>third person</u>.

- The **first person** uses the pronouns *I, me, we,* or *us.*
- The **second person** uses the pronoun *you.*
- The **third person** uses the pronouns *he, she, it, they,* or *them.*

Here's the scoop: Use the first person to write a personal story or an essay. Use the second person to give directions or instructions. Use the third person to tell a story or report an event.

Examples: <u>I</u> am looking for the Empire State Building's observatory.

<u>You</u> will need to take the elevator to the 86th floor.

<u>It</u> has a glass-enclosed area and a place to walk outside.

Write *1, 2,* or *3* to identify each sentence as written in the first, second, or third person.

1. _____ Astronomer Chang Heng invented the seismograph early in the second century.

2. _____ I was told to elevate and put ice on my sprained ankle for 24 hours.

3. _____ By the time you are 70 years old, your heart will have beaten about 2.5 billion times.

4. _____ People should eat five or more servings of fruits and vegetables each day.

5. _____ A numismatist collects money.

6. _____ I learned that the word *good-bye* is a shortened form of the expression *God be with you.*

7. _____ Jimmy said, "The Venus de Milo is a famous Greek statue of the goddess of love and beauty."

8. _____ You may not realize that a rubber squash ball can travel more than 90 miles (145 km) per hour when served.

Name _____ Date _____

Consistency in writing means that related numbers, genders, and tenses must agree with each other.

- The verb tense should be consistent throughout the description of an event or of a topic.

Example: The first commercial microwave <u>was produced</u> in 1947 and <u>was</u> as big as a refrigerator.

Avoid sentence time machines! If your sentence is about something in the past, use all past-tense verbs!

Circle the inconsistent word or words in each sentence. Then, write a replacement word or words that are consistent.

1. A biodegradable water bottle is made from corn and disappeared in about 80 days.

   _____

2. Jackrabbits have excellent hearing in part because they had long, funnel-shaped ears.

   _____

3. Mosquitoes are more attracted to people who wore dark clothing than people who wear light colors. _____

4. On May 10, 1869, the transcontinental railroad was completed, and bells ring in cities across the country. _____

5. Modern safety pins were patented in 1849 although they are used in the Bronze Age.

   _____

6. Most Americans did not use forks until the 1850s because spoons are more commonplace. _____

7. A fisherman has one of the most dangerous jobs in the country because he was always at sea. _____

8. Horses are social animals, and they gathered in herds for protection from predators.

   _____

Name _____ Date _____

Consistency in writing means that related numbers, genders, and tenses agree with each other.

• Use either first person, second person, or third person throughout a writing assignment, except when writing dialogue.

Example: A person may join a team, but they may not play in every game. (incorrect)

A person may join a team, but she may not play in every game. (correct)

Grammar experts, like myself, freak out when people use pronouns that don't match their subjects. Use the plural pronoun *they* with a plural subject, like *people*. Use *he* or *she* with a single subject, like *person*. It's your choice!

Write *1*, *2*, or *3* to identify each underlined word as written in the first, second, or third person. Then, rewrite the sentence correctly.

1. _____ A person should always wear a helmet when mountain biking, or you may be seriously hurt if you fall._____

    _____

2. _____ If a person has pet allergies, they should vacuum, dust, and keep the house as dander-free as possible. _____

    _____

3. _____ I like to practice my trumpet because you can pretend that you are Louis Armstrong. _____

    _____

4. _____ If anyone needs help remembering a phone number, you can try to memorize it in smaller chunks. _____

    _____

5. _____ Each chipmunk stuffed nuts, seeds, and berries into their cheeks and then carried the food home to store._____

    _____

6. _____ If you like writing songs and words, then one could be a composer and lyricist.

    _____

    _____

Name _____ Date _____

Parallel writing means that words in a series have a similar structure.

- When writing a list or a series of words, group similar ideas or items together.

Example: Monkeys like <u>to climb</u>, <u>jump</u>, and <u>bananas</u>. (unparallel writing)

Monkeys like <u>climbing</u>, <u>jumping</u>, and <u>eating</u> bananas. (parallel writing)

The parallel writing examples sound much better! That's because the list doesn't mix verbs with nouns!

- When writing a list of verbs, use the same form for all verbs.

Example: Hyenas like <u>hunting</u>, <u>eating</u>, and <u>to lie</u> in the shade.

Hyenas like <u>hunting</u>, <u>eating</u>, and <u>lying</u> in the shade.

In each sentence, circle the word or phrase that is not parallel. Then, write a replacement word or phrase that is parallel.

1. A good gymnast must have mental focus, strength, and balancing. _____

   _____

2. Important skills for playing basketball are dribbling the ball, shooting the ball, and defense. _____

   _____

3. Mercury's surface is like the moon; it has flat plains, steep cliffs, and marked by craters.

   _____

   _____

4. The nursing instructor explained how to set a broken arm, cleaning wounds, and how to check blood pressure. _____

   _____

5. The blue whale is an interesting creature for the following reasons: thick blubber, it is the world's largest mammal, and it weighs 3 tons (2.7 metric tons) at birth. _____

   _____

6. A pitcher plant attracts bugs with a scent of nectar, a half-closed lid, and colorful rim.

   _____

   _____

Name _____ Date _____

Review: Writing Consistency

Rewrite each sentence correctly.

1. The elephant, a very caring animal, are considered the fourth smartest animal in
   the world. _____

   _____

2. The most common type of color blindness are the inability to tell red from green.

   _____

   _____

3. A person may have his third molars, or wisdom teeth, but you may not be wise.

   _____

   _____

4. Crows living in big cities pick up fallen nuts from trees and placed them in the street so
   that vehicles driving by would crack them open. _____

   _____

   _____

5. Why do people has tonsils? _____

   _____

6. An octopus have the ability to unscrew a lid from a jar. _____

   _____

7. A group of zebras are called a zeal. _____

   _____

8. People suffering from anosmia has no sense of smell. _____

   _____

Science Factoid: The mongoose, a small animal that lives in Africa, Asia, and southwestern Europe, has a long body and short legs. Some types of mongoose use their speed, agility, and intelligence to attack venomous cobras.

A transitional word or phrase connects ideas and sentences.

- A **transitional word or phrase** is usually at the beginning of a sentence.

Example: A male horse is called a colt until about the age of four. <u>However</u>, a young female horse is called a filly.

Turn on your fan, because here's a hot tip! Always use a comma after a transitional word or phrase when it begins a sentence.

To connect ideas: *also, next, again, in addition, indeed*

To show a contrast: *however, but, yet, on the other hand, although*

To show a change in time: *next, after, before, then, later, first, second, again, now*

When giving an example: *for example, such as, for instance, in fact*

To show a conclusion: *in conclusion, finally, therefore*

To show a comparison: *in the same way, likewise, similarly*

Circle each transitional word or phrase.

Heroes come in all shapes and sizes—and species. Dolphins are known for their friendliness. In fact, dolphins have even been reported to protect people lost at sea. But, marine mammal experts had never heard of an inter-species recovery until this amazing rescue. Moko, a bottlenose dolphin, proved to be a guardian of two stranded whales in New Zealand. The two whales had repeatedly beached on a sandbar. A team of rescue workers had tried to help them for more than an hour. However, the workers were about to give up. Then, Moko arrived just in time. Somehow, the dolphin communicated with the whales and seemed to calm them. Next, she led them safely through the channel and out to sea. Recently, the whales have not been seen, but Moko still comes to play with swimmers in the bay.

Science Factoid: Have you ever wondered why your muscles become stiff after heavy exercise? Actually, during exercise, the circulatory system cannot supply the muscle fibers with enough oxygen. Consequently, the muscle cells produce a substance called lactic acid. Indeed, it is the buildup of lactic acid that causes stiffness and soreness.

Name _____ Date _____

Tone is one quality of writing style. Examples of tone include serious, informal, and humorous.

- Keep a consistent tone throughout your writing.
- Avoid slang in formal conversation or in formal writing.

The words *get* and *got* are too informal for a job request. See how the second example sounds more professional?

Examples: I'd like to get that office assistant job you got in the paper. (informal tone)

I would like to apply for the office assistant position advertised in *The Beachtown Beacon*. (formal tone)

For each sentence, underline the words or phrases that do not match the tone.

1. The judge asked the animal rescue worker to chill as she gave her emotional testimony about neglected puppies.

2. Ladies and gentleman, tonight Dr. James McLurkin will discuss his cool ideas on atoms and molecules.

3. The biologist's report states that the feeding tentacles and beak-like mouth of the giant squid grossed her out.

4. Bobby said, "Hey, Jimmy, let's perambulate through the playground, and then we can play in the dirt."

5. The news report described how the flight simulator data went down the tubes when the space laboratory's computers malfunctioned.

6. In this essay, I will prove that King Arthur was a cool dude even though some people think he never existed.

7. The pitcher's performance commenced with a curve ball, which he implemented by placing his middle finger on the seam.

8. This book explains what an awesome ruler Queen Elizabeth I of England was.

A **letter** is a written message that is sent to someone.

- A **formal letter** or **business letter** is used for important business.

If you're writing a business letter and you do not know the name of the person, use a general greeting like, "To Whom It May Concern" or "Dear Sir or Madam."

Write a three-paragraph letter to the chamber of commerce in a state capital or province, and request information about that region. Use the information below to help you. Use another sheet of paper if needed.

(your address) —

(today's date) —

(company name) —

(company address) —

(greeting) — Dear _____ :

(body of letter) —

(closing) — _____ ,

(your signature) —

Name _____ Date _____

A **letter** is a written message that is sent to someone.

• A **friendly letter** may be written to someone you know well.

Wait, there's more! You need to indent the first line of every paragraph in the body of a friendly letter.

Write a letter to a friend. Use the headings below to help you. Use another sheet of paper if needed.

(your address) ⎯⎡ _____
                    _____
(today's date) ⎯⎡ _____

(greeting) ⎯⎡ Dear _____ ,

(body of letter) ⎯⎡ _____
                    _____
                    _____
                    _____
                    _____
                    _____
                    _____
                    _____

(closing) ⎯⎡ Your friend,
(your signature) ⎯⎡ _____

History Factoid: Before postal stamps were used, the postage rate was written in the upper right corner of a letter. The first modern adhesive postage stamp was the British Penny Black, which showed an engraving of Queen Victoria. It was issued in 1840.

Name _____ Date _____

A <u>paragraph</u> is a group of sentences about one idea.

- A **topic sentence** begins each paragraph. It tells the reader what the paragraph is about.
- All of the sentences in the paragraph must relate to the topic sentence.

To indent a paragraph, start about five to seven spaces from the left margin before you start writing or typing. Yeah, that's easier to read!

Example:

topic sentence ⟶

<u>In 1851, a scientist named Jean Foucault used a pendulum to prove that Earth spins on its axis.</u> Foucault constructed a huge pendulum in Paris. The pendulum could swing in any direction. It had a bob that made a line in sand with each swing. After Foucault set the pendulum in a north–south motion, the lines in the sand appeared as if it was swinging in a clockwise direction. The lines proved that Earth was slowly turning.

Each topic sentence is underlined. Cross out the one sentence in each paragraph that is not about the topic sentence.

1. <u>Bicycles of the 1800s had very large front wheels.</u> These bikes, called penny-farthings, did not have gears like modern-day bikes. My mountain bike has gears. One turn of the pedal on the penny-farthing produced a large movement by the front wheel. This allowed the penny-farthing to travel faster than bikes with smaller front wheels. When gears are used on a modern-day bike, the bike does not need a large front wheel to travel fast.

2. <u>Although almost blind, the star-nosed mole is able to find food underwater.</u> Its amazing star-shaped nose allows the mole to smell underwater. Scientists tested this ability by using a trail of food. I don't know what kind of food they used. The moles blew tiny bubbles with their noses. Then, they sucked the bubbles back in. This allowed them to smell whatever the bubbles touched.

3. <u>Ptolemy, an ancient Greek astronomer in the second century, believed that Earth was the center of the universe and that the sun and the planets revolved around Earth.</u> He did not have access to accurate maps and measurement tools. It is difficult to be accurate if you don't have the right tools. In the 1500s, Copernicus, a mathematician and astronomer, found evidence that the sun was actually the center of our solar system.

A <u>paragraph</u> has supporting details.

- **Supporting details** give additional information about a topic.

Supporting details can be facts, examples, reasons, statistics, or even personal stories—anything that's an important addition to the topic sentence!

Example:

topic sentence →

    In the 1870s, a German businessman named Heinrich Schliemann searched for the lost city of Troy. First, he read Homer's *The Iliad*, which is about Troy and the Trojan War. The book gave him clues about the city's location. Then, he went to Turkey and began digging at Hissarlik. After 20 years, he found the ruins of nine cities built upon each other. Many people believe that one of these cities is the lost city of Troy.

supporting details →

Circle the topic sentence in each paragraph. Then, underline the supporting details.

1. Writing secret messages with invisible ink is easy. First, dip a cotton swab into a glass of lemon juice. Then, use the swab to lightly write a message on a white sheet of paper. Let the juice dry. To reveal the message, carefully hold the paper over a lightbulb that gives off heat. Watch your message become visible.

2. The parasitic wasp has a strange life cycle. First, the adult lays eggs inside a caterpillar. Then, these eggs develop into larvae that feed on the caterpillar's body fluids. Eventually, they crawl out of the caterpillar and spin silken cocoons. Interestingly, the caterpillar also spins a protective cocoon over the larvae. It stays close to the young wasps and watches over them.

3. Locks are used to raise and lower ships as they pass through different levels of water on canals or rivers. A lock has two gates to close a chamber. When a ship enters a chamber, the gates close, and workers fill the chamber with water or empty water from the chamber. The ship rises or lowers with the water level. When the water in the chamber is the same level as the next level, one gate opens and the ship continues its journey.

History Factoid: In 1572, astronomer Tycho Brahe discovered a new star that changed the way people thought about the universe. Today, we know that Brahe had seen a *supernova*, or exploding star, about 7,500 light years from Earth. Until Brahe's discovery, people thought that stars were permanently fixed in their places. Suddenly, people realized that the universe is continually changing.

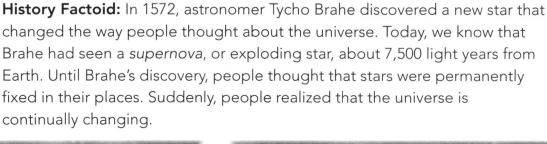

Write an outline to organize your ideas before writing an essay or a report.

- An **outline** must have a clear topic or thesis statement.
- A **thesis statement** tells the reader what the essay is about.

Example: Thesis Statement: A successful April Fools' Day prank requires skill.

You will need to write loads of thesis statements in middle school and high school. Remember that each supporting idea that follows the thesis statement should help to support your thesis.

I. First Main Idea: The person cannot suspect anything.

    A. Supporting Idea: Act as if everything was normal.

    B. Supporting Idea: Do not change your behavior or routine.

    C. Supporting Idea: Involve only friends who can keep a secret.

II. Second Main Idea: Play a prank only on someone who appreciates a joke.

    A. Supporting Idea: Never try to fool someone you do not know well.

    B. Supporting Idea: Make the prank or joke fit the person's sense of humor.

    C. Example: My friend tried to pull a joke on a stranger.

III. Third Main Idea: Never embarrass or upset someone.

    A. Supporting Idea: Do not bully or frighten anyone.

    B. Supporting Idea: Do not hurt anyone's feelings.

    C. Supporting Idea: A prank must never cause harm to someone.

IV. Conclusion: Anyone can learn to play a harmless joke.

On a separate sheet of paper, write a topic or thesis statement. Then, create an outline using the underlined headings in the example. Use your outline to write a short essay.

Know your audience.

- The **topic** should match the person or people who will read your writing.

Example: Topic: Understanding atmospheric pressure patterns

Interested audience: meteorologists

Less interested audience: ballet teachers

Different audiences are interested in different topics. For example, gremlins like gross and grungy topics, such as "Stuff stuck under your desk" or "Recycling smelly garbage."

Circle the audience that would most like to read about each topic.

1. Topic: Understanding a plane's canard wing

   a) airplane pilots   b) lifeguard   c) pastry chefs

2. Topic: Surviving in high elevations

   a) computer technicians   b) cyclists   c) mountain climbers

3. Topic: The history of French poodles

   a) heart surgeons   b) dog owners   c) landscapers

4. Topic: How to make vegetable soup

   a) young children   b) restaurant owners   c) astronauts

5. Topic: Spotting the rare Worcester's buttonquail

   a) fashion designers   b) lawyers   c) bird-watchers

6. Topic: Lawn mower repairs

   a) office workers   b) apartment owners   c) mechanics

Science Factoid: Sometimes, people's best ideas and topics come from their own dreams. In the mid-1800s, a German chemist named Kekulé was attempting to solve a puzzle. He knew which atoms were present in benzene, but how were they arranged to make a molecule? Then, in a dream, he saw snakes winding and turning. One of the snakes grabbed its own tail. Kekulé awoke with a start and drew the atoms arranged in a circle. This ring-shaped structure was the answer to his problem.

Capital letters begin sentences and proper nouns.

- Capitalize a proper noun, a person's name, and a person's initials.
- Capitalize a person's title.

Example: President Calvin Coolidge said that nothing in the world can take the place of persistence.

You don't just capitalize *president* any old time. It has to come before a person's name or in direct address. Aye-aye, Captain!

Circle each letter that should be capitalized.

1. thomas a. edison invented the kinetograph, a type of early movie camera.

2. u.s. general dwight d. eisenhower ordered the complete desegregation of the armed forces.

3. telephone inventor alexander graham bell's first words on a telephone were, "mr. watson, come here."

4. we saw the groundhog named punxsutawney phil at the Groundhog Day celebration near Pittsburgh, Pennsylvania.

5. andrew carnegie, once the richest man in the world, believed that education was the key to success.

6. the largest denomination of u.s. currency ever printed was the $100,000 gold certificate.

7. most historians agree that a Greek author named herodotus wrote the world's first history book more than 2,000 years ago.

8. until the year 1603, when james I became the king of England, Scotland had its own king.

9. *A Wrinkle in Time*, written by madeleine l'engle, has sold more than 6 million copies.

History Factoid: Dr. David Livingstone, a Scottish missionary, is recognized as one of the world's greatest explorers. In 1866, he set out to find the source of the Nile River. No one heard from Dr. Livingstone for several years. News reporter H. M. Stanley was sent to Africa by the owner of the newspaper to search for Dr. Livingstone. They finally met in the African village Ujiji in late 1871. However, Stanley's first words to Livingstone were probably not the famous question, "Dr. Livingstone, I presume?"

Name _____ Date _____

Capital letters begin sentences and proper nouns.

- Capitalize months of the year and days of the week.
- Capitalize the names of cities, states, countries, provinces, and planets.
- Capitalize the titles of books, movies, songs, magazines, and newspapers.

Grab a napkin, because here's a juicy tip! If the year includes the abbreviations *BC* or *AD*, capitalize them!

Example: On Tuesday, July 1, 1980, the song "O Canada" officially became Canada's national anthem.

Circle each letter that should be capitalized.

1. dogs may have been domesticated 12,000 years ago in the middle east.

2. the highest wind speed on earth was 231 miles (372 km) per hour, recorded in the state of new hampshire in 1934.

3. honolulu, hawaii, has a royal palace that served as the state capitol until 1969.

4. In tibet, it is good manners to stick out your tongue and hiss at someone.

5. On october 30, 1995, the province of quebec voted on whether to separate from canada.

6. On thursday, august 8, 1974, U.S. President Richard M. Nixon resigned as a result of the Watergate scandal.

7. The world's largest swimming pool is in algarrobo, chile, where it stretches for half of a mile (0.8 km).

8. On december 25, some people light a Yule log as a sign of goodwill and burn it through the 12 days of Christmas.

History Factoid: An unusual treasure was discovered in a Roman shipwreck off the Spanish coast. The sunken sailing ship from the first century AD could carry up to 400 tons (363 metric tons) of cargo. But, what cargo did it have? The ship contained more than 1,200 clay jars of garum, a bad-smelling fish sauce made from fish guts. Garum, an ancient delicacy, was used in many recipes. For archaeologists, the unusual wreck tells an important story about the trade between Rome and the Spanish port of Cadiz.

A <u>capital letter</u> begins the first word of a new quotation.

- The first word of a continuing quotation does not begin with a capital letter.

Examples: Abraham Lincoln said, "<u>T</u>hose who deny freedom to others deserve it not for themselves."

"<u>A</u>m I not destroying my enemies," asked Lincoln, "<u>w</u>hen I make friends of them?"

A quotation is not capitalized if it's part of a continuing sentence. So, you don't capitalize the word *when* in the second example. Now, that's tricky!

Circle each letter that should be capitalized.

1. "anything you can think of, you can create," said inventor van phillips, who created a type of artificial leg for athletes.

2. The first woman to swim the English Channel, Gertrude Ederle, said, "it could be done, it had to be done, and I did it."

3. "ask not what your country can do for you," said John F. Kennedy, "ask what you can do for your country."

4. Shortly after Christopher Columbus set sail, he wrote, "following the light of the sun, we left the Old World."

5. "a hunch," declared the director Frank Capra, "is creativity trying to tell you something."

6. Salvador Dali, a well-known painter, said, "ambition is a bird without wings."

7. About 30 years ago, well-known businessman Ken Olsen stated, "there is no reason anyone would want a computer in their home."

8. The record company that rejected the Beatles commented, "we don't like their sound, and guitar music is on the way out."

History Factoid: When Charles Townes was 10, he asked for an unusual Christmas gift—a drill. Townes always wanted to discover something. He eventually developed the idea behind the laser. At first, people didn't know what it could do. Townes said, "My view then was that it would touch many applications because it combined electronics and light." He was right. Laser technology is used today in surgery and many other important functions.

A <u>period</u> (.) means stop.

- Use a **period** at the end of a sentence.
- Use a period after most initials or abbreviations.

Example: In 1856, an 18-year-old chemist named William H. Perkin accidentally discovered the first artificial dye.

That works for me, because my full name is actually I. M. Gremlin. (Get it?)

Punctuate each sentence correctly by adding periods.

1. Water decreases friction because it acts as a lubricant

2. Capt C B "Sully" Sullenberger became famous on Jan 15, 2009, when he successfully landed an airplane, carrying 155 passengers, on New York's Hudson River.

3. Although no one called him Dr Imhotep, he advised Egypt's ancient royalty and was the first medical doctor known by name.

4. Before becoming the first African American Supreme Court justice, he was known as Thurgood Marshall, Esq , because *esquire* means *lawyer*

5. Residents of Washington, D C , were not allowed to vote in presidential elections until 1961

6. The sun's most northerly location, the Tropic of Cancer, is at 23° 30′ N latitude

7. In the early 1900s, Madam C J Walker started the Madam C J Walker Manufacturing Co and became the first self-made female millionaire.

8. Dr Christiaan Barnard performed the first human heart transplant on Dec 3, 1967

9. Ball bearings, invented by Jules P Suriray, were used in the world's first bicycle road race in 1869

10. The Babylonians wrapped their messages in thin sheets of clay and baked them

Name _____ Date _____

A sentence must end with end punctuation, such as a period (.), a question mark (?), or an exclamation point (!).

- Use a **question mark** (?) at the end of a question.
- Use an **exclamation point** (!) to show great excitement or emotion.

An exclamation point is usually used with a short sentence. If you use too many exclamation points, they will lose their impact. That's the truth! You better believe it! I'm not lying! (Maybe I'd better chill out?)

Examples: Did you know that the king cobra can reach 18 feet (5.5 m) in length?

I can't believe that the Mars rover *Spirit* is still working after six years!

Write a period, a question mark, or an exclamation point at the end of each sentence.

1. Parts of the Atacama Desert in Chile have not had rain since people began to keep records

2. I am shocked to hear that the average American uses 500 pounds (227 kg) of paper each year

3. Is it true that the United States has more bagpipe bands than Scotland

4. Hyenas may look similar to dogs, but they are related to cats

5. Vikings most likely did not wear helmets with horns

6. The amount of krill that a blue whale can eat every day is unbelievable

7. North America has more kinds of carnivorous plants than any other continent

8. Did Arthur pull Excalibur from a stone, or was the sword a gift from a mysterious lady

9. At birth, North American opossum babies look like tiny worms

10. Which British king owned the sailing ship the *Mary Rose*

Science Factoid: Did you know that scientists are trying to map all of the genes in the human body? According to the Human Genome Project, there are between 26,000 and 40,000 genes in a person's body. Once these are understood, scientists may help prevent many diseases. That's amazing!

A <u>comma</u> (,) means pause.

- Use **commas** to separate things in a series or in a list.

Example: <u>Platinum, osmium, and rhodium</u> are precious metals.

You should place a comma after each item in a list, but not after the last item!

- Use a comma between two or more adjectives.

Example: The camel spider is a predator with large, powerful jaws.

Punctuate each sentence correctly by adding commas.

1. If you are allergic to cats, you shouldn't hug kiss or cuddle your neighbor's kitten.

2. The femur tibia and fibula are the three bones in the human leg.

3. Microscopic single-celled organisms can thrive in a single drop of water.

4. The costly massive European airplane called the *Airbus A380* is the largest passenger airplane in the world.

5. Some people think of the appendix the coccyx and the tonsils as useless body parts.

6. The ichneumon fly has thin wings a long abdomen and jointed antennae.

7. Floods tsunamis fires or mudslides sometimes occur with earthquakes.

8. A canary-wing parakeet is a scrappy playful bird with a loud raspy voice.

History Factoid: In the mid-1700s, inventors were working on a problem: how to create a machine that could sew. Simply copying the movements of sewing by hand did not work. In the 1830s, Walter Hunt made an enormous, creative contribution. He developed a needle with an eye in the pointed end and a lockstitch. Others built on these ideas with such innovations as continuous thread on a spool, a pressure foot, and a cloth feed. By 1867, there were more than 800 patents on sewing machines and their parts, and the ready-to-wear clothing industry had begun.

Name _____ Date _____

A comma (,) means pause.

- Use a **comma** between the day of the week and the month and between the date and the year.
- Use a **comma** to separate cities, states, provinces, and countries.

Examples: The famous magician Harry Houdini was born on Tuesday, March 24, 1874.

North America's third largest Chinatown is located in Vancouver, British Columbia, Canada.

Get out your magnifying glass! Look carefully at the first example. There's *no* comma between March and 24. Good eye!

Punctuate each sentence correctly by adding commas.

1. The Wright brothers flew their airplane for the first time on December 17 1903.

2. Thomas Edison tested his electric lighting system in 25 New York City buildings on September 4 1882.

3. Martin Luther King Jr. made his famous "I Have a Dream" speech on Wednesday August 28 1963.

4. Born on October 27 1858, President Theodore Roosevelt is known for preserving American parks and recreational places.

5. Commander Neil Armstrong became the first person to walk on the moon on July 20 1969.

6. Because Venice Italy, is a city of canals, it is affected by flooding, ocean currents, and both water and air pollution.

7. Canada first hosted the Olympic Games in 1988 in Calgary Alberta.

8. The opera house in Sydney Australia, is famous for its concrete "shells" architecture.

History Factoid: Born on January 4, 1643, in Lincolnshire, England, Isaac Newton is one of the greatest scientists who ever lived. In his later years, he was in charge of the Royal Mint in London where money was produced. To stop counterfeiters, he ordered that coins be produced with grooved edges and a standardized weight and size.

A comma (,) means pause.

- When calling someone by name, use a **comma** after the name.
- Use a comma after *Yes* or *No* if the word starts the sentence.

Look at number 2. It's a tricky one! The sentence starts with the word *Yes* and then calls someone by name, so it gets two commas!

Examples: "Timothy, can you tell me what you get when you cross a parrot and a woodpecker?"

"Yes, you get a bird that talks in Morse code."

Punctuate each sentence correctly by adding commas.

1. "Miss Webb have you heard that a bag of water might keep houseflies away?"

2. "Yes Grace I have heard that people hang bags of water outside their homes and businesses."

3. "Ben do you know why hanging bags of water might drive flies away?"

4. "No but I guess that the bags somehow scare them away."

5. "Yes that is part of the reason, but other factors may be involved."

6. "Miss Webb is it because flies see their reflections in the water?"

7. "Rebecca you are right about the reflection, but light refraction is the main reason."

8. "Class does anyone know what *refraction* is?"

9. "Yes refraction means that instead of going in a normal, straight path, a ray of light bends and creates an optical illusion."

10. "Anthony you have just explained why a housefly might become confused and frightened by a hanging bag of water!"

Joke Break:
Patient: "Doctor, Doctor, I feel like a pin!"
Doctor: "Yes, I see your point."

A <u>comma</u> (,) means pause.

- Use a **comma** to separate a dependent and an independent clause.

  Example: Because spiders breathe air, the water spider carries a bubble of air to its underwater nest.

- Use a comma before a conjunction in a compound sentence.

  Example: Honeybees spend the winter in their hive, and they feed the larvae stored honey.

- A comma sometimes separates an appositive from the other parts of a sentence.

  Example: Ulysses S. Grant, the 18th president of the United States, was a Civil War general.

See how *the 18th president of the United States* tells you more about Grant? The words between the commas are an appositive. I'm positive!

Punctuate each sentence correctly by adding commas.

1. Even though fish live underwater they breathe oxygen.

2. Cumulus clouds are fluffy looking but cirrus clouds are wispy and are made of ice crystals.

3. While I am in Beijing I will visit Tiananmen Square the world's largest public square.

4. Even though most people assume that helium was first discovered on Earth it was actually first discovered in the sun in 1868.

5. The sooty shearwater a type of bird had the longest migration ever recorded.

6. The roaring forties may sound like a time in history but it is a position of latitude in the stormy Southern Ocean.

7. Jacques my next-door neighbor went to the Republic of Georgia last year and visited the world's deepest caves.

8. When your plane flies across the international date line from east to west you will need to set your watch ahead 24 hours.

Review: Commas

Punctuate each sentence correctly by adding commas.

1. Yuri Gagarin the first man in space spent years training for the mission but he spent only 108 minutes in space.

2. Unbelievably people did not know what the far side of the moon looked like until the late 20th century.

3. Yes the invention of the steam engine was inspired by a teakettle.

4. Sugar comes from sugar cane or it can be found in the roots of the sugar beet.

5. Can a horse see 350° almost a complete circle around his nose or is that a myth?

6. Glass is made by heating sand powdered limestone and sodium carbonate in a furnace.

7. When the oriental fire-bellied toad is frightened it turns on its back to display its bright red belly.

8. Ticks can spread Rocky Mountain spotted fever which is a severe illness.

9. A community of prairie dogs can consist of more than 1,000 animals and it can stretch underground for miles.

10. While stars and galaxies produce light they also produce radio waves.

11. "Mrs. Valdez are quasars the most distant objects in space?"

12. The highest sea cliffs in the world which are 3,600 feet (1,097 m) high are in Hawaii.

History Factoid: Does an island off the coast of Nova Scotia contain buried treasure? Legend tells that, in 1795, Daniel McGinnis found a freshly dug hole on Oak Island where something had been lowered down a shaft. Digging 30 feet (9 m), the boy and his friends found a layer of stones, layers of logs, and cut marks from a pick, but no treasure. Since then, people have spent millions of dollars digging hundreds of feet. Some think the pit holds William Shakespeare's hidden, unpublished manuscripts. But, nothing valuable has been found yet, and the longest treasure hunt in history continues.

Name _____ Date _____

An apostrophe (') shows ownership or where a letter or letters have been omitted.

- Use -'s for possessive singular nouns.
- Use -'s to make a symbol plural.
- Use an apostrophe to take the place of numbers in a date or a letter or letters in a word.

Example: With Len Ford's leadership, the '47 Michigan football team won every game.

You probably figured out that '47 means 1947. You can get away with leaving out numbers in dates or using contractions when you're speaking, but not as much when you write. 'Nuff said?

Punctuate each sentence correctly by adding apostrophes.

1. In 06, scientists announced the discovery of at least 52 new plant and animal species in Borneo.

2. Its a fact that each hair on your head grows about 6 inches (15 cm) each year.

3. Didnt you know that India gets its name from the Indus River?

4. Halleys comets last orbit was in 86, so it wont return to the inner solar system until 2061.

5. The first Web site was launched in 91.

6. How many ss are in the word *Mississippi*?

7. The worlds biggest web-spinning spider is the golden orb-weaver spider of South Africa.

8. If someone says youve dotted your *is* and crossed your *ts*, youve done a careful job.

9. The magnetar stars magnetic force is so strong that it could erase the information on a credit card at a distance of halfway to the moon.

10. Until the *TIROS I* was launched in 60, no weather satellites were orbiting Earth.

Science Factoid: Sir William Herschel was studying the stars through his telescope. He noticed that one star seemed a little different. The odd star was orbiting around the sun. This was not a star at all—but a new planet! Sir Herschel's accidental discovery in 1781 was named Uranus.

Name _____ Date _____

Quotation marks (" ") show the exact words of a speaker or emphasize special or technical words.

- A comma separates a quotation from the rest of the sentence.
- End punctuation is usually inside the quotation marks.

Don't tell me, "I don't know what a flying machine is!" The answer is "plane" and simple. Get it?

Examples: Orville Wright once remarked, "No flying machine will ever fly from New York to Paris."

Ketchup, once spelled "catsup" and "catchup," probably originated in the 1600s.

Punctuate each sentence correctly by adding quotation marks.

1. One man with courage makes a majority, said Andrew Jackson.

2. Everything has its beauty, observed the Chinese philosopher Confucius, but not everyone sees it.

3. Bernardo Atxaga said, To live is to change.

4. Victory goes to the player who makes the next-to-last mistake, explained a famous chess master.

5. The comedian said, When I was born, I was so surprised that I didn't talk for a year and a half!

6. A home run is called a grand slam when runners are on all bases.

7. Scientists determined that a bug can be brainwashed when they observed hairworm parasites causing grasshoppers to jump into water.

8. Salt crystals know what shape to grow into.

9. Sous-chef is the term used for a head chef's assistant.

Sports Factoid: When snow alternates from thawing to freezing, snow can form into hard, round lumps the size of corn kernels. Many skiers believe that this "corn snow" offers the best skiing for inexperienced skiers. These skiers usually tackle this type of snow early in the morning because the "kernels" of ice become wet and soggy as the temperature rises, and they no longer support weight.

Name _____ Date _____

A <u>colon</u> (:) can introduce a list.

- Use a **colon** when listing items in a series.
- Use a colon between hours and minutes to show time.

Examples: Here are some strange museums: The Dog Collar Museum, The British Lawnmower Museum, The Museum of Bad Art, and The Museum of Toilets.

The spacecraft *Phoenix* landed on Mars at 7:38 P.M. eastern standard time, on May 25, 2008.

Pay attention to this: A colon can mean, "Whoa! Here comes an important detail."

Punctuate each sentence correctly by adding colons.

1. When it is August 27, 1 00 P.M., in Seattle, Washington, it is August 28, 4 00 A.M. in Beijing, China.

2. Aerial photography and satellite imagery have been used for important purposes monitoring the environment, assessing natural disasters, and planning urban areas.

3. You should consider a number of things when buying a desktop computer the central processing unit, the memory, and the basic input/output system.

4. A basic first aid kit should contain adhesive bandages, gauze pads and tape, elastic bandages, and antiseptic cream.

5. The sun is strong between 10 00 A.M. and 4 00 P.M., so wear sunscreen and protective clothing if you are outdoors.

6. Some of the most endangered insects are members of the following species butterflies, dragonflies, moths, and beetles.

7. A Komodo dragon's diet consists of these favorites deer, pigs, water buffalo, and wild horses.

A semicolon (;) creates a pause longer than a comma.

- A **semicolon** can be used instead of a period or a conjunction to connect two closely related sentences.
- A semicolon can join two sentences that are separated by a transitional word or phrase.

Some transitional words are *however*, *therefore*, *in fact*, and *for example*; however, there are even more!

Examples: The Battle of Waterloo occurred in 1815; it was the end of Napoleon's Empire.

The Battle of Waterloo occurred in 1815; in fact, it ended Napoleon's Empire.

Punctuate each sentence correctly by adding semicolons.

1. Some snakes lay eggs others give birth to baby snakes.

2. Geographers divide the oceans into the Pacific, Atlantic, Indian, and Arctic smaller bodies of water are called seas, gulfs, and bays.

3. In 1867, the United States purchased Alaska from Russia for 7.2 million dollars this was an amazing bargain.

4. Until the late 1930s, toothbrushes were made with boar fur after this, nylon bristles were used.

5. Ancient Greeks used bleaches to change their hair color they identified red hair with courage.

6. The longest cave in the world is the Mammoth Cave system in Kentucky more than 350 miles (563 km) have been mapped.

7. California has a banana museum in fact, it has more than 17,000 banana-related items.

8. A type of mushroom in Brazil glows in the dark it is fluorescent green.

Science Factoid: Dragons in many cultures' folklore look almost alike; scientists wonder if they're based on a real animal. Komodo dragons, which live in Indonesia, certainly look the part; they have scaly skin and sharp teeth. They don't breathe fire, but one venomous bite can be deadly. They may be the basis of these legends.

A <u>hyphen</u> (–) can join two closely related words.

- A **hyphen** can join two or more words to form a compound adjective before a noun.
- A hyphen does not join two words if one ends with -*ly*.

This rule is a no-brainer, right? I mean, they don't call me a top-notch know-it-all for nothing!

Example: <u>Coal-burning</u> steam locomotives produced smoke, so <u>first-class</u> passenger cars were located as far away from the engine as possible.

Write hyphens where needed to form compound adjectives.

1. For a real bird's eye view, Dr. Julius Neubronner patented a camera that a pigeon could carry.

2. Growing in tropical climates, the ebony tree has black, fine grained wood used for canes and handles.

3. Experts agree that a one way street can allow traffic to flow more smoothly.

4. Pumpkins, a low calorie, high fiber squash, have been grown in North America for 5,000 years.

5. The sure footed mountain goat is related to antelopes and musk oxen.

6. Only recently have fast food restaurants begun to offer a variety of low fat items on their menus.

7. Did you know that left handed people make up about 10 percent of the world's population?

8. Before 1943, farmers earned extra income during the winter by adding hand wrapped paper labels to crayons.

Science Factoid: Everyone is aware of the awe-inspiring power of a volcanic eruption. Red-hot lava, mudslides, ash, and toxic gas are all dangerous. But, volcanic activity is also helpful. Volcanoes rebuild the ocean floor and create islands.

Name _____ Date _____

A <u>hyphen</u> (–) helps spell compound numbers and can create a new word by joining two words.

- Use **hyphens** to spell compound numbers from twenty-one to ninety-nine.
  Also, use a hyphen to spell a fraction.
- Use a hyphen to form a compound modifier, such as *11-year-old student*.

Would it be a top-notch idea to send a Mother's Day card to my great-great-grandmother's great-granddaughter?

Examples: During the Civil War, some women with <u>can-do</u> attitudes wanted to do more than supply food and clothing, nurse soldiers, and raise money.

About 700 women, <u>one-third</u> of whom were slaves, disguised themselves as men and fought in the armies.

Write hyphens where needed.

1. Twenty seven hours is the length of the longest movie in the world, *The Burning of the Red Lotus Temple*.

2. My great grandfather remembers when cars had wooden spoke wheels.

3. Deserts make up about one fifth of Earth's land surface.

4. About three quarters of Earth is covered by ocean water.

5. In Greek mythology, a centaur is one half man and one half horse.

6. Once a full time actor, Ronald Reagan became the 40th president of the United States.

7. With an all weather TV, you can watch your favorite shows stress free outdoors.

8. Most firefighters now have self contained airpacks in their helmets.

9. Twenty two square feet (two square m) of skin cover the average adult.

10. A half smoke is a popular type of sausage sold in Washington, D.C.

Science Factoid: Dolphins have been known to come to the aid of troubled swimmers. In 2007, a 15-foot-long great white shark attacked a 24-year-old surfer. Suddenly, a pod of dolphins appeared and made a protective ring around the surfer. As a result, the surfer survived.

Underlining, italics, and quotation marks (" ") are used to <u>punctuate titles</u>.

- **Underline** the titles of books, plays, movies, and TV programs when writing by hand. Use **italics** when typing.
- Use **quotation marks** for the titles of short stories, book chapters, poems, and songs.

> My favorite book is *Little Gnome on the Prairie!*

Example: The first chapter of *Alice's Adventures in Wonderland* is titled "Down the Rabbit Hole."

Underline or use quotation marks where needed.

1. Have you read about Mowgli in The Jungle Book by Rudyard Kipling?

2. Containing more than 1,300 pages, A Suitable Boy is a long novel set in India in the 1950s.

3. Robert Frost's poem, The Road Not Taken, is a metaphor for the decisions that we make in life.

4. Did you know Opal's dog in Because of Winn-Dixie is named after a supermarket?

5. My dad's favorite episode of the Star Trek TV series is The Trouble with Tribbles.

6. My brother likes to invent things, so I gave him the book Leonardo da Vinci: Giants of Science.

7. Henry Wadsworth Longfellow's poem, The Midnight Ride of Paul Revere, contains the famous words, "One, if by land, and two, if by sea."

8. In 1953, Elvis Presley stopped at a recording studio in Memphis, Tennessee, to record the song My Happiness for his mother.

History Factoid: When photography was introduced in 1839, photographs were processed separately before they could be added to a book. The first book illustrated with photographs, *The Pencil of Nature*, took two years to produce. Each of the hundreds of photographs had to be mounted individually. However, by the 1880s, new technology allowed publishers to use more photographs as well as other kinds of artwork.

Review: Punctuation Marks

Add the missing punctuation where needed.

1. Did you know that the popular holiday plant mistletoe grows as a parasite on trees

2. When a cat falls through the air it usually lands on its feet.

3. A newspaper first used aerial photography on June 26 1914, after a Massachusetts fire

4. Hollywood California, was called Hollywoodland in the 1940s but it was later shortened to Hollywood

5. An airplane can depart from New York at 4 00 P.M and arrive in California at 6 00 P.M because it crosses three time zones.

6. Mercury is very hot dry and airless scientists do not think the planet supports any life

7. Did you know that some people use the term alligator pears to refer to avocados

8. Some of the sports that do not use a time clock include baseball tennis golf and bowling.

9. The human body contains one of four major blood types A, B, AB and O.

10. Researchers are developing red purple yellow and white carrots.

11. In 10,000 BC, Earth's population was between 1 million and 10 million people

12. It was illegal for U S colonies to make their own coins they had to use only coins from Europe

13. The carousel, nicknamed the merry go round, originated about AD 500 riders sat in baskets as they spun around a pole.

14. Here are my favorite statues "The Thinker" "Venus de Milo" and "The Discus Thrower."

Science Factoid: A 1938 rumor said that the Great Wall of China could be seen from the moon. But, astronauts who landed on the moon in 1969 could not see it. The Great Wall is very big; its length is about 4,163 miles (6,700 km). However, it is narrow and the same color as its surroundings. Recent photographs from the International Space Station do show small sections of the wall, but it is not visible from the moon.

Posttest

Circle the letter of each correct answer.

1. Which is a run-on sentence?

   A. The *Viking I* took a picture of a rock formation on Mars that looked like a human face.

   B. When birds and bats eat plant seeds, the seeds pass through the digestive system of the animal, they may germinate far from the fruit-bearing tree.

   C. Many electronics use power even when they are turned off.

   D. Grapes were cultivated 6,000 years ago near the Caspian and Black seas.

2. Which is not a complete sentence?

   A. Americans spend more than $26 million every day at the movies.

   B. In Britain, the common term for umbrella is "brolly."

   C. Scientists discovered an ancient city in India that may date back to 7500 BC.

   D. The same number of bones in its neck as a human being.

3. What type of sentence is this?
Explain how coal releases chemical energy.

   A. interrogative

   B. declarative

   C. exclamatory

   D. imperative

4. Which sentence is in the present tense?

   A. The jumbo jet used 1 gallon (3.8 L) of fuel per second.

   B. Alektorophobia is a fear of chickens.

   C. Johnny Appleseed's real name was John Chapman.

   D. The Ensisheim meteorite fell to Earth on November 7, 1492.

5. Which is the simple subject of the sentence?
A spacecraft that spends all of its time in space doesn't need wings.

   A. time

   B. space

   C. spacecraft

   D. wings

6. Which is the direct object?
The tailor bird makes its nest by threading fibers through leaves.

   A. tailor

   B. bird

   C. nest

   D. fibers

Posttest

Circle the letter of each correct answer.

7. Which is the indirect object?
In the 1800s, some wealthy parents gave their babies pacifiers made of silver, called "silver soothers."

A. parents

B. gave

C. babies

D. pacifiers

8. What is the mistake in the sentence?
Fifty percent of the world's scientists nearly are assigned to military projects.

A. dangling participle

B. subject-verb agreement

C. double negative

D. misplaced modifier

9. Which words are adjectives?
Because sinus cavities are hollow, they warm the cold air.

A. sinus, cavities, cold

B. sinus, hollow, cold

C. sinus, hollow, warm, cold

D. cavities, cold, air

10. Which word is an adverb?
A person's five senses constantly notice information, which the brain processes.

A. person's

B. constantly

C. notice

D. processes

11. Which is the independent clause?
When a person has three consecutive strikes in bowling, it is called a turkey.

A. three consecutive strikes in bowling

B. When a person has three consecutive strikes in bowling

C. called a turkey

D. it is called a turkey

12. What is the mistake in the sentence?
Batting gloves, although not required equipment, is worn by players to protect their hands from blisters.

A. misplaced modifier

B. subject-verb agreement

C. verb-tense agreement

D. sentence fragment

Answer Key

Page 7
1. D; 2. C; 3. D; 4. B; 5. D; 6. C

Page 8
7. D; 8. B; 9. D; 10. B; 11. A;
12. B

Page 9
(CN = common noun,
PN = proper noun)
1. CN = steps; PN = Eiffel
Tower; 2. CN = worms, glaciers;
PN = Alaska; 3. CN = plates;
PN = Himalayan Mountains;
4. CN = people, tusks, horns;
PN = Middle Ages;
5. CN= stories, hare;
PN = Nanabozho;
6. CN = parts; PN = Atlantic
Ocean; 7. CN = businessman,
tourist, space; PN = Dennis Tito;
8. CN = years, chocolate;
PN = Mayas; 9. CN = dinosaur;
PN = Cretaceous Period, Inner
Mongolia; 10. CN = baseball;
PN = Jackie Robinson, African
American

Page 10
1. hailstone, melon; 2. Lungs,
thousands, tubes; 3. water,
temperature, freshwater;
4. heart, quarts, blood; 5. eyes,
squid, head; 6. teeth, beaver;
7. Boa constrictors, swimmers;
8. wave, airplane; 9. Dalmatians,
spots; 10. bumps, skin, heat

Page 11
1. Intelligence, intelligence;
2. Happiness; 3. contentment;
4. liberty, justice; 5. belief;
6. fear; 7. democracy;
8. softness

Page 12
1. a type of elastic tissue ➪
cartilage; 2. the world's tallest
building ➪ Burj Dubai;
3. ENIAC ➪ computer;
4. a spiral galaxy ➪ Milky Way;
5. a rescued lion ➪ Lusaka;
6. one-celled plants on
the ocean's surface ➪
phytoplankton; 7. a type of
salamander ➪ Mudpuppies;
8. Fido ➪ dog; 9. kuru ➪
disease; 10. a Russian well ➪
hole

Page 13
1. lions; 2. Radios; 3. tigers;
4. tornadoes; 5. pianos;
6. tortillas; 7. banjos; 8. hippos;
9. kangaroos; 10. volcanoes

Page 14
1. Eyelashes; 2. matches;
3. foxes; 4. leaves; 5. taxes;
6. churches; 7. boxes; 8. halves;
9. dresses; 10. knives

Page 15
1. countries; 2. cities; 3. libraries;
4. Mudpuppies; 5. ponies;
6. theories; 7. parties; 8. skies;
9. babies; 10. butterflies

Page 16
1. feet; 2. mice; 3. women;
4. deer; 5. Moose; 6. children;
7. oxen; 8. Geese; 9. fungi;
10. teeth

Page 17
1. boat's; 2. alligator's;
3. principal's; 4. country's;
5. book's; 6. teacher's; 7. child's;
8. Mr. Prasad's; 9. class's;
10. turkey's; 11. Canada's;
12. media's

Page 18
1. elephants, elephants';
2. mice, mice's; 3. children,
children's; 4. gorillas, gorillas';
5. feet, feet's; 6. owners,
owners'; 7. presidents,
presidents'; 8. leaves, leaves';
9. women, women's; 10. sheep,
sheep's

Page 19
1. eat; 2. rots; 3. forms; 4. live;
5. create; 6. crack; 7. eat;
8. contained; 9. climbed;
10. passes

Page 20
1. lies; 2. dream; 3. take,
remove; 4. run; 5. build;
6. occur; 7. measures; 8. speak;
9. grows, weighs; 10. live

Page 21
1. patented; 2. began;
3. bought; 4. popped;
5. brought; 6. weighed;
7. stood; 8. used; 9. developed;
10. grew

Page 22
1. will create; 2. will boost;
3. will hunt; 4. will erode;
5. will attract; 6. will grow;
7. will lose; 8. will expand;
9. will change; 10. will make

Page 23
1. flown; 2. occurred; 3. eaten;
4. devoured; 5. thought; 6. built;
7. frozen; 8. caught; 9. fallen;
10. known

Page 24
1.–10. were

Page 25

(N = noun, V = verb)

1. N = octopus, hearts; V = has;
2. N = spiders, hairs, legs, noise; V = rub; make; 3. N = scientists, Madagascar, fossil, amphibian; V = discovered;
4. N = elephants, calves, pounds, birth; V = weigh;
5. N = day, Venus, days, Earth; V = equals; 6. N = story, France, Cinderella, slippers; V = wears;
7. N = Nyctophobia, fear, darkness; V = is; 8. N = United States, percent, bottles, litter, garbage; V = become;
9. N = movie, King Kong, puppet; V = was;
10. N = Jackrabbits, plants, cacti; V = eat; 11. N = swans, babies, backs, water; V = carry;
12. N = snake, tree, tree; V = glides

Page 26

1. healthy, 10,000, every;
2. cool, moist; 3. constitutional;
4. tall, top; 5. upper; 6. One, two; 7. wide, 100, eucalyptus;
8. common, baking, inner, small, evergreen; 9. huge; 10. farm, feed, flour

Page 27

1. Cherokee; 2. Persian;
3. German; 4. Greek; 5. Viking;
6. Mayan; 7. U.S.; 8. French;
9. Siberian; 10. Canadian

Page 28

1. The, the, the; 2. The, the;
3. A, a, the; 4. The, an, the;
5. The, the, the, the; 6. The, the, the; 7. The, a, the; 8. The, the, the; 9. The, a, the; 10. The, a

Page 29

1. taller; 2. trickier; 3. more amazing; 4. lighter; 5. sturdier;
6. more colorful; 7. tastier;
8. more immense; 9. rainier;
10. more popular

Page 30

1. highest; 2. hottest; 3. newest;
4. hungriest; 5. most common;
6. largest; 7. most expensive;
8. most solitary; 9. most numerous; 10. most famous

Page 31

1. everywhere; 2. below;
3. carefully; 4. quickly;
5. increasingly; 6. gradually, down; 7. quite; 8. first;
9. accidentally; 10. outward, off

Page 32

1. once; 2. Usually; 3. Recently;
4. never; 5. sometimes; 6. often;
7. frequently; 8. Normally;
9. daily; 10. Tomorrow

Page 33

1. most slowly; 2. more enthusiastically; 3. more suddenly; 4. more severely;
5. more efficiently; 6. better;
7. deeper

Page 34

1. most interested; 2. correctly;
3. certainly; 4. brave;
5. accurately; 6. earliest;
7. more commonly; 8. boldly;
9. well; 10. successfully;
11. badly; 12. unsuccessful

Page 35

1. me; 2. I; 3. me; 4. I; 5. me;
6. me; 7. I; 8. I; 9. I; 10. me

Page 36

1. he; 2. her; 3. him; 4. her;
5. she; 6. He; 7. He; 8. her;
9. him; 10. her

Page 37

1. They dance to tell other bees where to find it.
2. They add it to drinking water to strengthen children's teeth.
3. They can identify and eat it in about 250 milliseconds.
4. They rained down in a Serbian town, which made them run for cover.
5. He (or She) showed us redwood trees that were 2,000 years old.
6. In South America, they smoke tarantulas over a fire before eating them.

Page 38

1. our, our, our; 2. their; 3. your;
4. our; 5. Their, their, their;
6. yours; 7. our; 8. Her; 9. his, his

Page 39

1. That, lobster; 2. These, hummingbirds; 3. These, islands; 4. These, coprolites;
5. Those, frogs; 6. That, elephant; 7. This, eel; 8. This, Big Ben; 9. That, sound

Page 40

1. him; 2. I; 3. them; 4. their;
5. them; 6. her; 7. we; 8. its, its;
9. yours; 10. We

Page 41

1. in; 2. of, in, to, of; 3. of, of, in;
4. for, in; 5. In, in, of; 6. through;
7. Over; 8. toward, with; 9. In, of, on; 10. of

Answer Key

Page 42
1. Among; 2. between;
3. between; 4. between;
5. among; 6. between;
7. Among

Page 43
(Objects of the preposition are in boldface.)
1. of the longest **fish**; in the **sea** below the **surface**
2. for **gold**; for the Latin *aurum*
3. by **Evangelista Torricelli**
4. In **1937**; over the **Pacific Ocean**
5. on **dust**; in the **atmosphere**
6. After 365 **days**, 6 **hours**, 9 **minutes**, and 9.54 **seconds**; around the **sun**
7. in the **Arctic**; on **mountaintops**
8. of unusual **mummies**; in the **bogs**, of **Ireland, Denmark**, and other European **countries**
9. In the **winter**; on icy **roads**
10. at the 1936 **Olympic Games**; in **Berlin, Germany**

Page 44
1. so; 2. but; 3. so; 4. and; 5. or;
6. and; 7. and; 8. but

Page 45
1. but; 2. nor; 3. or; 4. and;
5. but also; 6. or; 7. or; 8. or

Page 46
(conjunctions are in boldface)
1. **Because** the leaves that they eat are only an arm's length away;
2. **If** you look at London's Big Ben clock tower;
3. **So** they could have a closer trim;

4. **While** you may like baseball;
5. **Although** it may disgust you;
6. **Because** the giant yellowleg centipede of South America has potent venom;
7. **because** he wanted to break the world record;
8. **Because** the world's largest cupcake was so big;
9. **Because** a popcorn kernel's shell is waterproof;
10. **Although** their ears help radiate Africa's heat

Page 47
1. under; 2. in, from, of; 3. in, of, toward; 4. At, of; 5. of, in, across; 6. Although (S) and (CD);
7. both (CL), and (CL);
8. and (CD); 9. Because (S);
10. Because (S)

Page 48
Definitions will vary but may include: 1. *de-*, to move downward; 2. *sub-*, under the water; 3. *re-*, to do again; 4. *im-*, not likely to be true; 5. *pre-*, of a time before written history;
6. *pro-*, the state of being guarded; 7. *mis-*, to be wrong

Page 49
1. -less; 2. -ians; 3. -tic; 4. -hood;
5. -er; 6. -able; 7. -ary; 8. -tion;
9. -ing; 10. -ade

Page 50
C (complete) for 2, 5, 6, 8, 9, and 10; *I* (incomplete) for 1, 3, 4, and 7

Page 51
1. period; 2. period; 3. period;
4. question mark; 5. period;
6. period; 7. exclamation point;
8. question mark;
9. question mark;
10. exclamation point

Page 52
1. Liquids; 2. airplane;
3. Great Barrier Reef;
4. people; 5. Hypocretin;
6. car; 7. Department of Defense; 8. civilizations;
9. surfaces; 10. reptile

Page 53
1. sees; 2. produces; 3. saw;
4. cools; 5. eat; 6. measures;
7. work; 8. dive; 9. found;
10. flow

Page 54
1. CS = Queen Cleopatra, Roman General Marc Antony;
CP = married, maintained;
2. CP = was lost on an Alpine glacier, was found 44 years later in a different location;
3. CP = developed an interest in mountain gorillas, studied them for years;
4. CS = Hurricanes, typhoons, tropical cyclones;
5. CP = exists in a dry environment, is more salty than the ocean;
6. CP = turns the skin a bronze color, damages the body's organs;
7. CP = built, flew an airplane with the world's largest wingspan;
8. CP = invented, then mass-produced the bendable straw;

9. CS = Spring peepers, American robins;
10. CP = laid her eggs, coiled her body around the eggs to keep them warm

Page 55
1. meat; 2. insects, larvae, fish … spiders; 3. species; 4. buds; 5. thorns; 6. home; 7. thorns, buds; 8. ants; 9. larvae; 10. buds

Page 56
1. cubs; 2. him; 3. me; 4. Trojans; 5. sweethearts; 6. cubs; 7. Abraham Lincoln, him; 8. female; 9. women; 10. wife

Page 57
R (run-on) for 4, 5, and 6

Page 58
1. C; 2. C; 3. C; 4. F; 5. C; 6. C; 7. F; 8. C; 9. F; 10. F

Page 59
1. R; 2. C; 3. F; 4. C; 5. F; 6. R; 7. C; 8. F; 9. C; 10. F; 11. F; 12. R

Page 60
1. It's; 2. its; 3. its, its; 4. its; 5. It's; 6. it's, its, its; 7. its; 8. its

Page 61
1. are; 2. use; 3. travels; 4. say; 5. is; 6. do; 7. spins; 8. churns; 9. acts; 10. contains

Page 62
(S = subject, V = verb)
1. vibrations (S), are (V); 2. insects (S), see (V); 3. army (S), was (V); 4. flock (S), contains (V); 5. bus (S), is (V); 6. waves (S), create (V); 7. group (S), is (V); 8. leaves (S), are (V); 9. chalk (S), is (V); 10. changes (S), occur (V)

Page 63
(S = subject, V = verb)
1. feeling, tingling (S), tells (V); 2. either (S), is (V); 3. weather, drought (S), contribute (V); 4. Raven, jay (S), eats (V); 5. Luke, Amanda (S), are (V); 6. Mahatma Gandhi, Dr. Martin Luther King Jr. (S), was (V); 7. amethyst, opal (S), is (V); 8. mother, father (S), tell (V); 9. Viruses, bacteria (S), are (V); 10. python, boa (S), have (V)

Page 64
(S = subject, V = verb)
1. no one (S), was (V); 2. few (S), are (V), all (S), eat (V); 3. Many (S), think (V); 4. anyone (S), wonders (V); 5. each (S), shows (V); 6. each (S), is (V); 7. each (S), is (V); 8. none (S), is (V); 9. Some (S), attach (V); 10. some (S), think (V)

Page 65
1. There is; 2. There is; 3. There are; 4. There is; 5. There are; 6. There are; 7. There are; 8. There are; 9. There was; 10. There were

Page 66
(S = subject, P = pronoun, V = verb)
1. condor (S), she (P), produces (V); 2. Mouthbreeders (S), they (P), shelter (V); 3. fish (S), they (P), make (V); 4. Both (S), they (P), have (V);. 5. Metal (S), it (P), feels (V); 6. One (S), She (P), is (V); 7. Everyone (S), he (P), wants (V); 8. Elephants (S), they (P), are (V)

Page 67
1. carries; 2. is; 3. weighs; 4. is; 5. is; 6. believe; 7. was; 8. she; 9. washes; 10. he; 11. it; 12. they

Page 68
1. well; 2. well; 3. good; 4. well; 5. good; 6. well

Page 69
1. bad; 2. bad; 3. badly; 4. badly; 5. bad; 6. badly; 7. badly; 8. bad; 9. bad

Page 70
C (correct) for 2 and 3. 1. not never; 4. aren't no; 5. never … no; 6. aren't never; 7. No … can't; 8. don't never

Page 71
1. lies; 2. lie; 3. set; 4. set; 5. laid; 6. set; 7. sit

Page 72
1. effect; 2. affects; 3. affects; 4. effect; 5. effect; 6. affect; 7. affects; 8. effect; 9. affect

Page 73
1. except; 2. raise; 3. rise; 4. rise; 5. rise; 6. accept; 7. accept; 8. raise

Answer Key

Page 74
1. beet; 2. byte; 3. hoarse;
4. grown; 5. pedal; 6. deer;
7. course; 8. night; 9. days;
10. fleas

Page 75
1. quite, quiet; 2. pores;
3. shone; 4. than; 5. already;
6. Where; 7. lose;
8. complementary; 9. whether

Page 76
(I = independent,
D = dependent)

1. Human saliva contains the enzyme amylase (I); which helps to digest food (D)

2. A jackrabbit . . . can leap about 45 miles (72 km) per hour (I); which is actually a hare (D)

3. A full-grown adult has 32 teeth (I); which includes four wisdom teeth (D)

4. Many bacteria have tails (I); which are called flagella (D)

5. Some cockroaches hiss (I); when they fight (D)

6. Organisms need water (I); because it helps them live and grow (D)

7. A golf ball can travel faster at high altitudes (I); where there is less air resistance (D).

8. When mountain snows were heavy (D); mail delivered from Missouri to California could take 12 to 16 days (I)

9. To lure predators away from their nests (D); both the adult curlew and the plover pretend to be injured (I)

10. Although it may look like medication (D); a placebo is really a sugar pill (I)

Page 77
1. which; 2. which; 3. who;
4. who; 5. that; 6. which;
7. which; 8. which

Page 78
1–5. Answers will vary.

Page 79
1–6. Answers will vary.

Page 80
Answers will vary but may include:

1. The Olympic Games have many different events, but some Olympic sports are unusual.
2. The ancient Olympic Games were supposed to build diplomacy, and the games honored Zeus.
3. Beach volleyball was not a sport in the ancient Olympic Games, but it was added at the 1996 Atlanta games.
4. Pole-vaulting started when men used poles to cross canals, but distance was more important than height.
5. The first Olympic torch relay was part of the summer games in 1936; it was added to the winter games in 1952.

Page 81
1. The sunflower tracks the sun's movement. This phenomenon is called heliotropism. 2. Argentina grows sunflowers. The sunflower seed is Argentina's most important product. 3. Russia grows the most sunflowers. The sunflower is its national flower.
4. Sunflowers are very fast growing. In fact, they can grow up to 15 feet (4.5 m) tall.
5. Some experts believed that sunflowers first grew in what is now the eastern United States. They were grown 4,000 to 5,000 years ago.

Page 82
Answers will vary but may include:

1. Today, sunflowers are a practical crop with many uses; sunflowers are among the top U.S. cash crops.
2. Sunflower products include cooking oil; sunflower seeds are high in protein.
3. Sunflower roots can grow deep into polluted water systems; they are able to take out large amounts of uranium and other toxic metals.
4. Sunflowers should be planted in sunny areas; they need well-drained soil.
5. Sunflowers are salt resistant; they grow on coastal beaches and dunes.

Page 83
1–7. Answers will vary.

Page 84
Answers will vary but may include:

1. Paper money is inexpensive to make; it costs only pennies to make one American dollar.
2. Buy shoes in the afternoon. This is when a person's feet have expanded in size.

3. Sinus cavities are hollow. They lie behind the forehead, eyes, and cheeks.

4. Answers will vary.

5. Viruses in the body are hard to kill, but laser light is a new approach.

6. Answers will vary.

7. Answers will vary.

Page 85

1. Cordless tools have been sold only since the 1960s.

2. Because symptoms may be minor, parents may notice a child's colorblindness only when he is learning colors.

3. Penicillin was discovered accidentally by Alexander Fleming in 1928.

4. On a sunny day, people can start a fire using only a magnifying lens and tinder.

5. A male platypus has sharp spurs on its rear feet that secrete venom.

6. Only one person in every 1,000 can see the indigo part of the light spectrum.

7. An ancient Roman artifact that is more than 2,000 years old is in the museum.

8. Nocturnal vampire bats in South America prey on cows and horses that are often asleep.

9. The Hope Diamond, which was once owned by King Louis XIV of France, is on display at the Smithsonian Institution.

10. The golden wedding anniversary is celebrated only after 50 years of marriage.

Page 86

Answers will vary but may include:

1. Stubby the dog received many medals after traveling with soldiers into battle.

2. Stroking with their wings as if flying underwater, puffins hunt small fish.

3. While waiting for a donor heart, the patient received the Jarvik-7 artificial heart.

4. Before a supernova occurs, the star's gravity compresses its core.

5. Crawling above the ground at night, earthworms consume soil.

Page 87

1. 3; 2. 1; 3. 2; 4. 3; 5. 3; 6. 1; 7. 3; 8. 2

Page 88

Answers will vary but may include:

1. disappeared ⇨ disappears;
2. had ⇨ have; 3. wore ⇨ wear;
4. ring ⇨ rang; 5. are ⇨ were;
6. are ⇨ were; 7. was ⇨ is;
8. gathered ⇨ gather

Page 89

Answers will vary but may include:

1. A person (3), you (2), you (2), You should always wear a helmet when mountain biking, or you may be seriously hurt if you fall.

2. A person (3), they (3), If people have pet allergies, they should vacuum, dust, and keep the house as dander-free as possible.

3. I (1), you (2), you (2), I like to practice my trumpet because I can pretend that I am Louis Armstrong.

4. anyone (3), you (2), If you need help remembering a phone number, you can try to memorize it in smaller chunks.

5. Each (3), their (3), Chipmunks stuffed nuts, seeds, and berries into their cheeks and then carried the food home to store.

6. you (2), one (3), If you like writing songs and words, then you could be a composer and lyricist.

Page 90

Answers will vary but may include:

1. balancing ⇨ balance;
2. defense ⇨ playing defense;
3. marked by craters ⇨ craters;
4. cleaning wounds ⇨ how to clean wounds; 5. thick blubber ⇨ it has thick blubber;
6. colorful rim ⇨ a colorful rim

Answer Key

Page 91
Answers will vary but may include:
1. The elephant, a very caring animal, is considered the fourth smartest animal in the world.
2. The most common type of color blindness is the inability to tell red from green.
3. A person may have his third molars, or wisdom teeth, but he may not be wise.
4. Crows living in big cities pick up fallen nuts from trees and place them in the street so that vehicles driving by will crack them open.
5. Why do people have tonsils?
6. An octopus has the ability to unscrew a lid from a jar.
7. A group of zebras is called a zeal.
8. People suffering from anosmia have no sense of smell.

Page 92
In fact; But; However; Then; Somehow; Next; Recently

Page 93
1. to chill; 2. cool; 3. grossed her out; 4. perambulate; 5. went down the tubes; 6. cool dude; 7. performance commenced, implemented; 8. awesome

Page 94
Answers will vary.

Page 95
Answers will vary.

Page 96
1. My mountain bike has gears.
2. I don't know what kind of food they used.
3. It is difficult to be accurate if you don't have the right tools.

Page 97
The first sentence in each paragraph should be circled. Answers for supporting details will vary but may include:
1. Sentences 2, 3, 4, and 5
2. Sentences 2, 3, and 4
3. Sentences 2, 3, 4, and 5

Page 98
1. Answers will vary.

Page 99
1. A; 2. C; 3. B; 4. B; 5. C; 6. C

Page 100
1. Thomas A. Edison; 2. U.S. General Dwight D. Eisenhower; 3. Telephone; Alexander Graham Bell's; Mr. Watson; 4. We; Punxsatawney Phil; 5. Andrew Carnegie; 6. The; U.S.; 7. Most; Herodotus; 8. Until; James; King; 9. Madeleine L' Engle

Page 101
1. Dogs, Middle East;
2. The, Earth, New Hampshire;
3. Honolulu, Hawaii; 4. Tibet;
5. October, Quebec, Canada;
6. Thursday, August;
7. Algarrobo, Chile;
8. December

Page 102
1. Anything, Van Phillips; 2. It;
3. Ask, Ask; 4. Following; 5. A;
6. Ambition; 7. There; 8. We

Page 103
1. Water decreases friction because it acts as a lubricant.
2. Capt. C. B. "Sully" Sullenberger became famous on Jan. 15, 2009, when he successfully landed an airplane, carrying 155 passengers, on New York's Hudson River.
3. Although no one called him Dr. Imhotep, he advised Egypt's ancient royalty and was the first medical doctor known by name.
4. Before becoming the first African American Supreme Court justice, he was known as Thurgood Marshall, Esq., because esquire means lawyer.
5. Residents of Washington, D.C., were not allowed to vote in presidential elections until 1961.
6. The sun's most northerly location, the Tropic of Cancer, is at 23° 30' N. latitude.
7. In the early 1900s, Madam C. J. Walker started the Madam C. J. Walker Manufacturing Co. and became the first self-made female millionaire.
8. Dr. Christiaan Barnard performed the first human heart transplant on Dec. 3, 1967.
9. Ball bearings, invented by Jules P. Suriray, were used in the world's first bicycle road race in 1869.
10. The Babylonians wrapped their messages in thin sheets of clay and baked them.

Page 104

1. period; 2. exclamation point;
3. question mark; 4. period;
5. period; 6. exclamation point
or period; 7. period; 8. question
mark; 9. period; 10. question
mark

Page 105

1. If you are allergic to cats, you shouldn't hug, kiss, or cuddle your neighbor's kitten.
2. The femur, tibia, and fibula are the three bones in the human leg.
3. Microscopic, single-celled organisms can thrive in a single drop of water.
4. The costly, massive European airplane called the *Airbus A380* is the largest passenger airplane in the world.
5. Some people think of the appendix, the coccyx, and the tonsils as useless body parts.
6. The ichneumon fly has thin wings, a long abdomen, and jointed antennae.
7. Floods, tsunamis, fires, or mudslides sometimes occur with earthquakes.
8. A canary-wing parakeet is a scrappy, playful bird with a loud, raspy voice.

Page 106

1. December 17, 1903;
2. September 4, 1882;
3. Wednesday, August 28, 1963;
4. October 27, 1858;
5. July 20, 1969; 6. Venice, Italy;
7. Calgary, Alberta; 8. Sydney, Australia

Page 107

1. Miss Webb,; 2. Yes, Grace,;
3. Ben,; 4. No,; 5. Yes,; 6. Miss Webb,; 7. Rebecca,; 8. Class,;
9. Yes,; 10. Anthony,

Page 108

1. underwater,; 2. looking,;
3. Beijing,; Square,; 4. Earth,;
5. shearwater,; bird,; 6. history,;
7. Jacques,; neighbor,; 8. west,

Page 109

1. Gagarin,; space,; mission,;
2. Unbelievably,; 3. Yes,;
4. cane,; 5. 350°,; nose,;
6. sand,; limestone,;
7. frightened, bright,; 8. fever,;
9. animals,; 10. light,;
11. Valdez,; 12. world, high,

Page 110

1. '06; 2. It's; 3. Didn't;
4. Halley's, comet's, '86 won't,;
5. '91; 6. s's; 7. world's;
8. you've, *i*'s, *t*'s, you've; 9. star's;
10. '60

Page 111

1. "One man with courage makes a majority," said Andrew Jackson.
2. "Everything has its beauty," observed the Chinese philosopher Confucius, "but not everyone sees it."
3. Bernardo Atxaga said, "To live is to change."
4. "Victory goes to the player who makes the next-to-last mistake," explained a famous chess master.
5. The comedian said, "When I was born, I was so surprised that I didn't talk for a year and a half!"

6. A home run is called a "grand slam" when runners are on all bases.
7. Scientists determined that a bug can be "brainwashed" when they observed hairworm parasites causing grasshoppers to jump into water.
8. Salt crystals "know" what shape to grow into.
9. "Sous-chef" is the term used for a head chef's assistant.

Page 112

1. 1:00, 4:00; 2. purposes:;
3. computer:; 4. contain:;
5. 10:00, 4:00; 6. species:;
7. favorites:

Page 113

Semicolons should be written between each word pair.

1. eggs; others
2. Arctic; smaller
3. dollars; this
4. fur; after
5. color; they
6. Kentucky; more
7. museum; in
8. dark; it

Page 114

1. birds-eye; 2. fine-grained;
3. one-way; 4. low-calorie, high-fiber; 5. sure-footed;
6. fast-food, low-fat;
7. left-handed; 8. hand-wrapped

Page 115
1. Twenty-seven;
2. great-grandfather, wooden-spoke; 3. one-fifth;
4. three-quarters; 5. one-half, one-half; 6. full-time;
7. all-weather, stress-free;
8. self-contained; 9. Twenty-two;
10. half-smoke

Page 116
1. The Jungle Book; 2. A Suitable Boy; 3. "The Road Not Taken"; 4. Because of Winn-Dixie; 5. Star Trek, "The Trouble with Tribbles"; 6. Leonardo da Vinci: Giants of Science; 7. "The Midnight Ride of Paul Revere";
8. "My Happiness"

Page 117
1. Did you know that the popular holiday plant, mistletoe, grows as a parasite on trees?

2. When a cat falls through the air, it usually lands on its feet.

3. A newspaper first used aerial photography on June 26, 1914, after a Massachusetts fire.

4. Hollywood, California, was called "Hollywoodland" in the 1940s, but it was later shortened to "Hollywood."

5. An airplane can depart from New York at 4:00 P.M. and arrive in California at 6:00 P.M. because it crosses three time zones.

6. Mercury is very hot, dry, and airless; scientists do not think the planet supports any life. (This sentence also may be written as two sentences or joined by a comma and a conjunction.)

7. Did you know that some people use the term "alligator pears" to refer to avocados?

8. Some of the sports that do not use a time clock include: baseball, tennis, golf, and bowling.

9. The human body contains one of four major blood types: A, B, AB, and O.

10. Researchers are developing red, purple, yellow, and white carrots.

11. In 10,000 BC, Earth's population was between 1 million and 10 million people.

12. It was illegal for U.S. colonies to make their own coins; they had to use only coins from Europe. (This sentence also may be written as two sentences or joined by a comma and a conjunction.)

13. The carousel, nicknamed the "merry-go-round," originated about AD 500, and riders sat in baskets as they spun around a pole. (This sentence also may be written as two sentences or joined by a semicolon.)

14. Here are my favorite statues: "The Thinker," "Venus de Milo," and "The Discus Thrower."

Page 118
1. B; 2. D; 3. D; 4. B; 5. C; 6. C

Page 119
7. C; 8. D; 9. B; 10. B; 11. D; 12. B